alpha
books

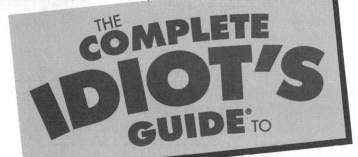

THE
COMPLETE
IDIOT'S
GUIDE® TO

Volunteering

for Teens

by **Preston Gralla**

201 West 103rd Street
Indianapolis, IN 46290

A Pearson Education Company

This book is dedicated to my brother Eliot, who devoted his life to helping others. Countless people in this world are alive because of him, and countless others lead a better existence because of the good he's done. He enriched everyone who ever came into contact with him, and the lives of thousands of others whom he never met. His life may have been a passing breath, but his good works live forever.

Copyright © 2001 by Preston Gralla

THE COMPLETE IDIOT'S GUIDE TO and Design are registered trademarks of Pearson Education.

International Standard Book Number: 0-02-864166-3
Library of Congress Catalog Card Number: Available upon request.

03   02   01   8   7   6   5   4   3   2   1

Interpretation of the printing code: The rightmost number of the first series of numbers is the year of the book's printing; the rightmost number of the second series of numbers is the number of the book's printing. For example, a printing code of 01-1 shows that the first printing occurred in 2001.

Printed in the United States of America

Note: This publication contains the opinions and ideas of its author. It is intended to provide helpful and informative material on the subject matter covered. It is sold with the understanding that the author and publisher are not engaged in rendering professional services in the book. If the reader requires personal assistance or advice, a competent professional should be consulted.

The author and publisher specifically disclaim any responsibility for any liability, loss, or risk, personal or otherwise, which is incurred as a consequence, directly or indirectly, of the use and application of any of the contents of this book.

Publisher
Marie Butler-Knight

Product Manager
Phil Kitchel

Managing Editor
Jennifer Chisholm

Senior Acquisitions Editor
Renee Wilmeth

Development/Copy Editor
Lynn Northrup

Production Editor
Billy Fields

Illustrator
Brian Moyer

Cover Designer
Dan Armstrong

Book Designer
Gary Adair

Indexer
Angie Bess

Layout/Proofreading
Angela Calvert
Mary Hunt
Natashia Rardin

Contents at a Glance

Part 4: Beyond Volunteering   173

Appendixes

Contents

Introduction

There's a lot of good that needs doing in the world, and too few people to do it. There are the hungry to feed, the elderly to care for, the needy to help, animals to shelter, the public's safety to protect, the arts to be nurtured ... the list goes on and on.

That's where you come in. You have energy, youth, and idealism. You have good ideas. You have time (well, let's not get carried away here—if you're like most of us, you probably don't have as much time as you'd like). And so you'd like to volunteer to help others.

How do you go about volunteering? What should you know before getting started? What kind of volunteering is right for you? What will you do when you volunteer? How do you find your dream volunteer opportunity?

The Complete Idiot's Guide to Volunteering for Teens answers all these questions and more. Whether you've never volunteered before or you're a seasoned pro, you'll find a lot here to help you. It's a comprehensive guide to everything you need to know about volunteering.

How to Use This Book

You can read this book from cover to cover or just dip into it as you need to. To help you find the information you need, I've organized the book into four parts, each of which focuses on a different aspect of volunteering:

Part 1, "Getting Started with Volunteering," prepares you for any kind of volunteer experience. You'll start with the basics—the reasons why you should consider volunteering. You'll learn all the benefits of volunteering and what you should expect when you volunteer. You'll learn about the different kinds of volunteer experiences open to you and find out how to match yourself to your ideal volunteer opportunity. I'll also provide a worksheet to help you decide where to volunteer.

Part 2, "How to Prepare for Your Volunteer Experience," gets you ready once you've decided to volunteer. You'll learn what will be expected of you when you volunteer, how to make sure that you have enough time for volunteering, and how to check out an organization before applying so you know it's right for you. And you'll learn important skills and techniques for getting your dream volunteering job—how to write a resume, how to have a great interview, and other important things you need to know.

Part 3, "Finding Volunteering Experiences," tells you how to find the right volunteer opportunity for you. It's a chapter-by-chapter rundown on every category of volunteering you can imagine: from volunteering to help the elderly and the needy to caring for animals; from volunteering for public safety, the environment, and the arts to building better neighborhoods and volunteering for literacy and education. You'll learn what kind of work you'll do for each area of volunteering, find out any special issues you should know for each kind of volunteering, see how you can find volunteering opportunities near you, and get a complete resource guide to volunteering opportunities.

Part 4, "Beyond Volunteering," tells you how you can go solo and create your own volunteering experience, and how to pursue a career in social work or with nonprofit institutions.

In addition, you'll find two appendixes packed with contact information, Web sites, and some books on volunteering that you might find helpful.

Extras

To help you get the inside track on volunteering, I also give you some helpful tips, resources, cautions, and other bits of information. You'll find them in these boxes:

Helping Hands

These boxes give you tips for helping you get the best volunteering opportunity possible.

It's the Pits

Look in these boxes for cautions you should keep in mind when figuring out where and how you want to volunteer.

Inside Scoop

These boxes offer interesting tidbits of information about volunteering that you probably never knew.

Information Station

Check these boxes for resources such as Web sites and books that can help you get more information about volunteering.

Acknowledgments

Thanks go to many people for helping with this book. I'd like to thank acquisitions editor Renee Wilmeth for trusting me with the book, and development/copy editor Lynn Northrup for whipping it into shape. Also thanks to the production team at Pearson Education for all their efforts behind the scenes to turn this manuscript into a book.

As always, thanks to my agent Stuart Krichevsky. And many thanks to my wife, Lydia, and my two children, Gabe and Mia. Most of all, though, thanks go to the guiding spirit of this book, Eliot.

Trademarks

All terms mentioned in this book that are known to be or are suspected of being trademarks or service marks have been appropriately capitalized. Alpha Books and Pearson Education, cannot attest to the accuracy of this information. Use of a term in this book should not be regarded as affecting the validity of any trademark or service mark.

Part 1
Getting Started with Volunteering

Ready to become a volunteer? Great! Then let's begin.

Whether you're a long-time volunteer or haven't yet donated any time, you'll learn a lot in this section. You'll find out why you should volunteer and what you'll get out of it. You'll learn about the different types of volunteer experiences you can have, and discover how to match yourself to the right volunteering opportunity.

And for those who like Top Ten lists—there's something for you as well—a list of 10 questions you should ask yourself before volunteering.

Chapter 1

Pass It On: How to Get Started with Volunteering

In This Chapter

✧ Discovering all the reasons you should volunteer

✧ Uncovering the benefits of volunteering

✧ How volunteering can help you in college and beyond

✧ What to expect when you volunteer

✧ Some pitfalls of volunteering

Volunteering can be one of the great experiences of a lifetime. It's a chance to do good in the world and make a difference, to meet new people, to try things you've never imagined, and to have fun.

But how do you get started? What are the basic things you'll need to know? How can you decide whether you should even volunteer? In this chapter, you'll learn the basics of volunteering. You'll find out the benefits of volunteering, you'll see what you'll get out of volunteering, and you'll find out what will be expected of you when you volunteer. So volunteer a little time for yourself and curl up with this chapter—you're about to find out how to get started on something that can help change the world—and yourself as well.

Why Should You Volunteer?

So you're in the midst of deciding whether you want to be a volunteer. You know what you're giving up by volunteering— free time (and so less time for spending at the mall), TV time (no loss there, although you can always tape *Buffy the Vampire Slayer* if you need to), and family time (no jokes now, I know there's an upside to that as well).

Well, if you're thinking of volunteering, you're not alone. An estimated 50 percent of all teens volunteer every year. That means 13.3 *million* teens, giving up 1.8 *billion* hours a year to help others. That's a whole lot of people and a whole lot of hours. So you're in good company!

Why do so many teens bother to volunteer? Why do they give up so much of their free time?

There are plenty of reasons to give up your time to help:

✧ **You want to do good for the world.** There's a lot that's wrong in the world. Just turn on the TV news or read your daily newspaper. You can't run for president, or issue an edict proclaiming world peace. But you can volunteer at one of many organizations that will help do good in the world.

✧ **You want to do good for individuals.** It's not just the big issues that need fixing. People do, too. For a few hours a week, you can make a huge difference in someone's life by doing simple things like bringing meals, tutoring, helping run errands, or simply providing companionship.

✧ **You want to meet new people.** One of the best ways to meet new people and make friends is to volunteer. People who volunteer tend to be friendly and outgoing, and it's a great way to meet people you otherwise might never meet.

✧ **You want to try new things.** School, home, friends … it can all seem a bit routine after a while. Volunteering can change that. You'll get to do new things you've never done before—like working in a zoo, animal shelter, or a state park, or other neat stuff.

✧ **You're trying out for a career.** Think you might want to work as a veterinarian? In health care? To help save the environment? Then volunteer now in an animal shelter, hospital, or park—it'll go a long way toward helping you decide what you eventually want to do with your life.

✧ **You feel a responsibility for others.** Many people feel a responsibility to share their good fortune with others. There's no better way than to volunteer.

Helping Hands

If you're looking for a place to volunteer, often the simplest place to begin is at home. Ask your parents and siblings if they know of any place or anyone that needs help. You'll be surprised at how often you'll find volunteer experiences that way.

✧ **It can help you get into college.** When colleges decide who to accept and who to turn down, they look at everything a person has done, not just at the school record. Doing meaningful volunteer work can help you get a leg up on getting into college.

✧ **It's a high school graduation requirement.** An estimated 16 percent of high schools across the country require that students spend time doing volunteer work in order to graduate. Your school may be included in that 16 percent.

What You'll Get from Volunteering

So now you know all the reasons you should volunteer. Great. But is it really worth all the time you'll put in? Yes, you volunteer because you want to help others, but there's probably a small voice inside of you asking, "What's in it for me?"

Don't feel guilty that the little voice is there—we all have it. And don't try to ignore it, either. Unless you answer the question, you're less likely to become a volunteer. And if you do volunteer and don't answer the voice, you're less likely to give volunteering your all.

In fact, there's a lot in volunteering for you. Read on to find out about all the benefits you'll gain.

It Will Help Your Future Career

As I've mentioned, volunteering is a great way to try out different careers. You'll get a taste of what real working life is like in whatever career you're interested in. Some people actually spend years of their lives trying out different careers. You can do it in a matter of months. Talk about saving time!

If you happen to know what career you want to choose, volunteering will give you a leg up on getting a job. For example, if you're interested in work as an environmental activist, and your potential employer sees that you've already spent time doing the work as a volunteer, you'll be more likely to get the job.

Even if your volunteer work isn't related to your career, volunteering will help you get a job. When an employer sees that you have real-world experience, and that you're willing to work even if you're not getting paid (just make sure he pays you for your real job!), you're more likely to be put at the top of the list.

It's the Pits

Don't do volunteer work just because you think it will look good on your resume. You'll be unhappy, the organization you volunteer for will be unhappy, and the people you're supposed to help will be unhappy. And spreading unhappiness is no way to get ahead in life.

It Will Enhance Your Sense of Self

The more you help others, the more you help yourself. Helping other people and volunteering gives you a greater sense of self-worth and independence. The sense that you can actually change the world for the better makes you more connected with the world, and more optimistic. And you'll discover that if you can help change the world, you'll also have the power to change your own life. All in all, you'll find that volunteering can give you a new outlook on life, one in which you believe that you can take control of your present and future—and do good in the bargain as well.

It Will Prepare You for the Future

The things you do and the skills you acquire volunteering are a lot like the things you'll do later in life: such as working with people you've never met before, working as part of a team, learning cooperation, or doing fund-raising. The earlier you learn these skills, the better, and when you volunteer, you'll learn them in spades.

It Will Teach You Leadership Skills

When you volunteer, you learn to take charge of things. As a start, you have to decide where you want to volunteer, and then you have to apply and get the volunteering job. And often when you volunteer you must be a self-starter—a lot of what you do you may have to decide on your own. Those are all quick ways to build up leadership skills.

Inside Scoop

Former President Bill Clinton often did volunteer work as a teen. He helped organize charity events to raise money for his church. I'm not saying that's why he became president, but it certainly taught him how to work with others, and the value of spending time bettering the world.

It Will Improve Your World

Tired of dirty streets? Of unsafe neighborhoods? Of poorly treated stray animals? You can help solve all those problems. Volunteer and you'll make a difference, not just in the world, but in your neighborhood. You can make your neighborhood and town a safer, better place to live.

You'll Have Fun

Surprise! It's a whole lot of fun to volunteer. Doing new things, meeting new people, getting the satisfaction of knowing that you're making a difference in the world … those are just some of the reasons that you'll have a great time when you volunteer.

What to Expect When You Volunteer

Perhaps you've never volunteered before and aren't quite sure what to expect. When you get to your volunteer job, will life be one big party—people dancing in the aisles to hip-hop and the music of the latest pop diva? Or will you come across dour-faced people whose attitude toward life seem to be that if you're going to do good deeds, you better do them with as straight a face as possible? Will you be expected to bear the entire burden of volunteering yourself? Or will you be patted on the head and told to sit in the corner, because teens should be seen rather than heard?

Luckily, you'll probably come across none of that. Instead, you'll most likely meet well-meaning people who, like you, want to do good. Perhaps they'll be a bit harried, because generally, do-good organizations tend to be understaffed and overcommitted.

And what will be expected of you? First and foremost, to show up and to show up on time. One of the biggest problems facing organizations using volunteers is that too often people simply don't show up, or don't show up when they're supposed to.

You'll also be expected to be something of a self-starter ~ least after you've been volunteering for a while ~ tainly get training and advice, but the~ times you'll be expected to w~ you've been doing ~ volunteer~

10

If you're ties are a computer. find volunt across the c

Be aware that just because people work at an organization that does good in the world and needs volunteers, that doesn't mean that they're going to be perfect. They're just as imperfect as the rest of us. (Okay, not including you, of course, since we both know you're as close to perfection as they come!)

So there's a chance that you may come across problems when you volunteer. You may be surprised to find out that some people may resent you—they'll think that you're just a kid and not serious about the work you're doing—or they may resent you because you're still young and free and they have to work for a living. (Just remind them what homework is like and maybe they'll lighten up.)

It's most likely, though, that you'll have a great volunteer experience, that you'll do good while having fun, meeting new people, expanding your horizons, and making a better future for yourself as well as the world. What could be better?

The Least You Need to Know

✧ Volunteering helps you try out different careers while you're helping others and the world.

Volunteering can help you get into college and get a
od job after you graduate.

teering is a great way to learn leadership skills and
work with others toward common goals.

asic requirement for volunteering is that you
be on time.

Chapter 2

Choosing the Best Volunteering Experience

In This Chapter

✧ Learning what kinds of help volunteer organizations lend to others

✧ Finding out what categories of volunteer organizations need help

✧ Ten important questions you should ask yourself before deciding where to volunteer

✧ The match game: finding out what volunteer experience is right for you

✧ Using a simple worksheet to help decide on the best volunteer experience

There's a lot that needs to get done in this world, and a lot of organizations devoted to making things better. That means that there are a lot of places to choose from when you want to volunteer.

But which volunteer experience is right for you? Should you help at a homeless shelter or with your local police department? At a zoo or an art museum? Cleaning up your neighborhood or building housing for people? And what kind of organization is the right one—a small, local one, or a large organization that's part of an even larger national organization? And should you volunteer during the summer or during the school year?

These are just some of the things you need to figure out before choosing the right organization where you'll volunteer. Don't be put off by all this, because it's easy to find the right volunteering experience for you. I'll tell you how in this chapter.

What Type of Volunteering Experiences Are There?

When it comes to volunteering, there's good news: There's a volunteering experience for you. No matter your interests, your personality, and where you live, if you want to help others, you'll be able to find the right experience for you.

As you'll see in this section, there's a wide range of kinds of types of volunteering you can do, from helping animals to aiding the environment, to helping the elderly and more. And there are many different ways you can help, such as by bringing meals to people, fund-raising, working on political campaigns, or directly helping others. Read on to find out all about what kind of experiences are open to you.

What Categories of Volunteering Can You Do?

No matter your interests and curiosities, the world is open to you when you volunteer. There are more volunteering experiences than you can imagine. Here's a list of the most common kinds of volunteering you can do:

✧ **Volunteering in hospitals, nursing homes, and health institutions.** If you want to help the elderly or people who are ill, you'll find many places to volunteer. You'll do things such as reading to children in hospitals to delivering meals to the elderly and everything in between. For more information, turn to Chapter 5, "Volunteering in Hospitals and Health Organizations."

✧ **Volunteering in shelters and with the elderly.** Shelters for the homeless, including homeless women and children, always need volunteers, as do places that serve the elderly. It can be something as simple as helping serve a Thanksgiving dinner, or more substantial, such as tutoring a homeless child. For more information, turn to Chapter 6, "Helping the Elderly and Caring for the Needy."

It's the Pits

If you're interested in volunteering in a hospital, be aware that there may be age limits on volunteers. You may have to be over a certain age before you're allowed to volunteer.

✧ **Volunteering at zoos and animal shelters.** Animal lovers will be pleased to know that there are a lot of volunteer opportunities available. Animal shelters, pounds, and zoos often need helpers. For more information, turn to Chapter 7, "Volunteering at Zoos and Animal Shelters."

✧ **Volunteering for the environment.** If you care about the health of the environment, you'll find many volunteering opportunities. It can be anything from a local community group organizing a cleanup of a local park, to helping out an organization wanting to help solve the problem of global warming. For more information, turn to Chapter 8, "Volunteering for the Environment."

✧ **Volunteering to build better neighborhoods.** There's a saying that goes, "Think globally, act locally." If you want to help make your neighborhood or another neighborhood a better place, you can volunteer with neighborhood organizations. You might work to make sure that new construction doesn't harm neighborhoods, or help build new housing for people. For more information, turn to Chapter 9, "Volunteering to Build Better Neighborhoods."

✧ **Volunteering for the arts.** If you're interested in the arts, there are more than enough volunteer opportunities for you. You can help out at local museums, create neighborhood murals, and much more. For more information, turn to Chapter 10, "Volunteering for the Arts and in Museums."

Inside Scoop

My brother Eliot spent much of his life volunteering—particularly raising money to help the hungry. He got his start volunteering at local political campaigns at a very young age, doing things like folding letters and licking envelopes—and loving every second of it. He made a difference, and that was just a beginning to his time as a volunteer.

✧ **Volunteering in politics and government.** Everyone likes to complain about problems with politicians and the government. Guess what? As a volunteer, you can actually do something about them! You can work on political campaigns, or in some cases you can even help out in your local government offices. For more information, turn to Chapter 11, "Volunteering in Politics and Government."

✧ **Volunteering for literacy and education.** A surprising number of people have trouble reading—even adults. And many kids and even teens can use help with tutoring. You can volunteer as a tutor and to help kids and teens with homework. For more information, turn to Chapter 12, "Volunteering for Literacy and Education."

✧ **Volunteering in public safety, police, and fire departments.** You may not realize this, but tens of thousands of teens every year volunteer in police offices, fire departments, and other public safety organizations. You can be one of the more than 45,000 teen Police Explorers who help out police or fire departments. For more information, turn to Chapter 13, "Volunteering in Public Safety."

Helping Hands

If you'd like to help out at police or fire departments but are worried about the danger, don't be. You won't be allowed to go into burning buildings or arrest criminals. But there are many other things you can do, such as helping to find missing people and maintaining fire-fighting equipment.

15

Ten Questions to Ask Yourself Before Volunteering

Think volunteering is for you? Great! But before you jump in with both feet, you want to make sure that you're really, truly, absolutely ready for it. So before you volunteer, ask yourself these 10 questions:

1. **Why am I volunteering?** Sounds like a simple question, doesn't it? You may be surprised, though, at how tough it may be to answer. Are you volunteering out of guilt, or because you think it's the right thing to do— but deep down, you're not sure it's something you *want* to do? Are you volunteering because you want to meet new people? Because you want to change the world?

2. **How much time do I have?** Are you on the run from morning until night? Are you trying to become a prima ballerina as well as a soccer star and cheerleader—all while holding down a job and spending some serious time hanging out with friends? Be realistic about how much time you can devote to volunteering, and see how it will fit into your schedule.

3. **What do I enjoy doing?** One of the great things about volunteering is that you can spend time helping others while doing things you like to do. Do you enjoy painting? Then you can probably volunteer to help create a neighborhood mural. Enjoy taking photographs? No doubt, there will be a chance to help an organization by taking photos for them.

4. **What would I like to learn?** Another great benefit of volunteering: You can use it to do things and learn things you've always wished you could do. Want to go mountain climbing? There's probably an environmental volunteer experience right up your alley—err, mountain.

5. **Am I a loner or do I prefer groups?** Some volunteering allows you to do things on your own, while others

require that you work closely with people. Think about how you're happiest and then look for that kind of experience.

6. **Do I want to volunteer during the school year or during the summer?** Some places need volunteers year-round, while others only require that you volunteer during the summer. Decide which time is best for you.

7. **What do I want to get out of volunteering?** Do you want to try out a future career? Want to feel the satisfaction that you've made a difference in the world? Have something good to put on your college application? Before you decide what volunteering you want to do, make sure you know what you expect to gain from the experience.

8. **What things do I hate doing?** Volunteering should be a fun, productive experience—not something you dread going to every day. Do you hate sitting in an office and doing paperwork? Then make sure you tell that to any organization you're considering joining. Can't stand doing physical labor? Cleaning up a local river isn't for you.

9. **What type of people do I want to be with?** At some organizations, you'll work mainly with young people—and at others, you'll work primarily with older people. Would you rather work in a daycare center or a home for the elderly? Do you want to work with people like you or different from you?

10. **What issues are most important to me?** Do you care the most about environmental issues such as global warming? About the safety of your town or city? About the plight of the poor and the homeless? About how poorly stray animals are treated? Think about the issues that are most important to you, then look for a volunteering experience to help solve that problem.

17

Matching Yourself to the Right Volunteering Experience

Once you've answered these 10 questions, you've got a great handle on what volunteering experience is best for you. But how do you get from here to there? Answering questions is one thing, but helping match yourself to the right volunteering experience is another.

In this section, you'll learn how to match yourself to the right volunteering experience, taking into account who you are, what your interests are, and how much time you have to devote to helping others.

Inside Scoop

Volunteering doesn't mean that you have to join an organization. There are many ways you can work on your own to make the world a better place. For information on how to do that, turn to Chapter 14, "Creating Your Own Volunteering Experience."

Write Down Your Answers to the 10 Questions

To match yourself to the right volunteering experience, write down your answers to each of the 10 questions from the previous section. Make sure each answer is more than a single sentence, but don't turn it into an essay. What you want to end up with is a single sheet of paper with your answers to all 10 questions.

Once you've written down your answers, walk away for a while. Wait before reading them again, so that you can get a fresh look. Take your time. Check out MTV. Take a nap. Pick an argument with your younger brother or sister. OK? Feel refreshed now? Time to get back to the sheet.

Now take out a clean sheet of paper. Based on everything you read from your answers, write a single paragraph that describes the kind of volunteering you want to do. Make sure to include this basic information:

✧ What category of volunteering you want to do (such as helping with animals or helping the environment)

✧ The amount of time you can devote to volunteering, and when you want to volunteer

✧ A brief description of what the organization should be like and how you fit in (for example, what kind of people are in the organization and whether you'll work in a group or alone)

Great! You now have a good starting point to match yourself to the right volunteer experience.

Describe Your Perfect Volunteer Group

So you've written out a paragraph describing in what way you'd like to volunteer, and how you'd like to fit into the organization. Time for the next step—describe the perfect volunteer group.

What kind of group should it be—a local group or part of a larger state or national organization? Should it focus on only local issues or on global concerns? How large should the organization be—would you prefer to be part of a large group, or are you the kind of person who wants to be part of a smaller crowd?

You should now have a sheet of paper with two paragraphs on it. The top describes the kind of volunteering that you'd like to do, and the bottom describes the ideal group where you'd like to volunteer. You're almost done!

Information Station

When looking for a place to volunteer, you may be surprised that you won't have to look that far afield. Often, the best place to start is by asking family and friends. You'll be surprised at how often they can point you to the right group.

Your Worksheet for Deciding on Where to Volunteer

One more step and you're ready to go. As a quick way to help decide what kind of volunteer experience is best for you, use the following worksheet. Along with your answers to the 10 questions earlier in the chapter and the two paragraphs you just wrote, it'll help you find the perfect volunteer experience for you.

Choosing the Right Volunteer Experience

Type of Organization

Type of work (working with animals, public safety, etc.)?

_____

Size of organization (small, medium, or large)?

_____

Local only or part of state and national organization?

_____

New or established organization?

_____

How You'll Work There

Work alone or in groups?

_____

Self-directed or under direct supervision?

_____

Time You'll Spend

During the school year or the summer?

_____

Hours per week you're willing to donate?

_____

Volunteer daily, weekly, or on a changeable basis?

_____

Other Issues

What's the work environment like (formal or informal)?

_____

What kind of people will you be working with?

_____

How does it match what you love doing?

_____

How does it match what you'd like to learn?

_____

Will it help with college or your planned career?

_____

Final thoughts (Describe anything not included on this worksheet.):

_____

_____

By now you should have a good idea what volunteer experience and organization are right for you. For information on how to get the volunteering job once you've found the right one, turn to Chapter 4, "Getting Your Dream Volunteering Job."

The Least You Need to Know

✧ Before choosing any single volunteer experience, learn about the many different kinds of opportunities open to you.

✧ Ask yourself why you want to be a volunteer, and then choose your organization based on that.

✧ Figure out how much time you can devote to volunteering and make sure you choose an opportunity that works with your schedule.

✧ Choose an organization that matches your personal needs, such as working alone or in groups.

✧ Write paragraphs describing your perfect volunteer experience, and the perfect organization, and then match the organization to what you've described.

✧ Fill out the worksheet in this chapter before deciding where to volunteer. And fill out the worksheet for each opportunity, as a way to help you choose among them.

Part 2

How to Prepare for Your Volunteer Experience

On your marks, get set … yes, you're at the starting line. It's time to prepare for your volunteer experience. No, that doesn't mean you need to put on your track suit and start doing hamstring stretches. But it does mean it's time to get ready.

In this part, you'll learn all the basics of getting ready to volunteer. You'll find out what will be expected of you when you volunteer, you'll get the inside track on how to decide where you want to apply, and you'll learn how to check out a volunteer organization before applying so you know it's the right one for you. You'll also get advice on writing a resume and making a great impression at the interview, as well as tons of tips on how to get that volunteer dream job!

Chapter 3

Preparing for Your Volunteering Experience

In This Chapter

✧ Learning about the different kinds of things you'll do as a volunteer

✧ Making sure that you don't overextend yourself, and that volunteering fits into your schedule

✧ What an organization will expect of you

✧ Checking out newsletters, Web sites, and budgets to get the rundown on an organization

✧ Talking to other volunteers to find out what they think of a volunteer organization

The idea of volunteering may be scary or exciting to you, particularly if you've never done it before. And particularly if you've never volunteered before, you probably don't have a clue what to expect and want to check out an organization before deciding whether to volunteer there.

In this chapter, you'll learn what to expect from a volunteering experience and the different kinds of things you'll do when volunteering. You'll find out how to make sure volunteering fits into your schedule. You'll learn what an organization expects from its volunteers. And finally, you'll discover how you can check out a group before volunteering to make sure that it's the right group for you. So before you decide on a group that deserves your time and energy, read this chapter first.

What Types of Volunteer Experiences Are Open to You?

In the last chapter, you learned about the different kinds of work you can do when volunteering—things like helping out at animal shelters, daycare centers, political campaigns, or police departments.

But when you're thinking of volunteering, it's not only the kind of work you can do you need to think about. It's also the different kinds of things you'll do as a volunteer— working in an office, let's say, or riding in a police car. In order to prepare for your volunteer experience you need to know about those kinds of things. If you're going to work in an office, for example, it's a good idea to learn how to type ahead of time.

So what kind of volunteering experiences are open to you? They're as wide and varied as the world. Here's a brief run-down on the main kinds, what you need to know about them, and how to prepare for each.

✧ **Office work.** Organizations need all kinds of office work done. There are many simple things, like typing letters or using an office computer for all the different kinds of things that office computers can do. (No video games, please—after all, you're at work!) And there are other things as well, such as helping organize the office to keep it running smoothly. If you want to do office work, brush up on your computer skills and perfect your telephone voice.

✦ **Fund-raising.** Count on it: Any organization that needs volunteers also needs to raise funds. Nonprofit and similar organizations are almost always short of cash. That means they're always doing fund-raising of some sort. You might make phone calls asking for money or help organize a big fancy fund-raising event. To do this kind of work you need to be well organized, so get yourself a daily planner or calendar and practice organizing your time.

Inside Scoop

You've heard the term "nonprofit institution" a lot but may not know what it means. Generally speaking, it's a place that consciously doesn't make a profit on its work—any leftover money is put back into helping people.

✦ **Newsletter writing.** Organizations—especially nonprofit organizations—need to stay in touch with people who support them, and with the public. Because of this, they often need people to work on their newsletters— everything from writing to taking pictures to laying them out and getting them printed. For this kind of work you need solid writing skills and a good grasp of grammar, so practice now.

✦ **Public relations.** Nonprofit and similar organizations often need to get publicity. They need to get it to draw attention to a problem they want to solve, or to get people to attend a fund-raising event. To help, you might write press releases, hand out flyers, or talk to editors, reporters, and TV and radio stations. For this kind of work you should be comfortable dealing with people you don't know, and you should be an effective communicator as well.

✧ **Hands-on work.** This covers just about everything you can imagine. It means actually doing the work itself, such as providing daycare, delivering meals, cleaning up a park, bathing animals, or helping at a hospital. It can even mean riding in a police car for eight hours on a weekend. One way or another, though, it means getting your hands dirty. If you want to do this kind of work, you should be the kind of person who likes to pitch right in and is comfortable working by yourself at times.

Inside Scoop

The most up-to-date organizations don't just publish newsletters—they publish and maintain sites on the World Wide Web. And they often need savvy volunteers to help them. In fact, this is one way that volunteering can lead to a part-time paying job.

Keep Track of Your Time—Check Your Schedule First

So much to do and learn, so little time. If you're like a lot of people (me included!), there are many more things you'd like to do than you actually *can* do. Sometimes you spread yourself too thin. This is one of the most common problems for organizations that need volunteers. Many people want to volunteer, and so they sign up. And at first they're there every day, on time and enthusiastic. But then one day leads to another, and one week leads to another … and volunteers start showing up late. Then they skip a day or two. Then a week or two. And then they're gone.

When this happens, the organization is usually better off if you'd never volunteered than if you start and then quit or only show up occasionally. In fact, many organizations will tell you it's their number one problem with volunteers. They'd be happier if fewer people volunteered, but if everyone who volunteered actually showed up.

Don't become a volunteer burnout case—you'll only hurt yourself and the people you're trying to help. Before you agree to volunteer, check your schedule. That means more than just giving a quick glance. It means plotting out your schedule on a calendar, or better yet, a day planner that includes places for every hour of every day of the week where you can write down what you'll be doing. To start, for each day of the week block out your school time, time you spend with family and friends, time for sports and hobbies, and time for anything else that you do. Now take a look at what's left.

It's the Pits

Don't assume that you can just fill in any holes in your schedule with volunteering. Things don't work that way. Life goes on; things always come up. You'll most likely be able to volunteer far less than you think you can.

I'd recommend that to start, don't agree to volunteer more than about five hours a week, and certainly less if you need to. You can break it up any way you want—an hour five days a week, two-and-a-half hours twice a week, and so on. But the point is, start small, with an amount of time that you know you can easily give. You can always increase the number of hours to volunteer if it's working out well.

What Will Be Expected of You?

Volunteering isn't like hanging out at home or with your friends. It isn't even like spending time at school or in after-school activities. When you volunteer, you're entering the adult world, and you'll be expected to act like one. No, that doesn't mean you'll have to start listening to Frank Sinatra and complaining to your friends about your current medical condition. But it *does* mean you'll have to be more conscious of how you present yourself and how the world perceives you. Even more important, it means you have to be responsible in certain ways to help the organization and the people you're trying to help.

Keep in mind that while there are many personal reasons why you're volunteering, the focus when you volunteer shouldn't be on *you*. It's on the people or animals you're trying to help, and on the organization that's letting you do the volunteering. The volunteer organization will have a number of expectations about you and the way you behave, and if you keep your focus on them, not on yourself, it'll be easy to meet them.

Enough sermonizing—let's get on to business. Here are the main things that will be expected of you when you volunteer:

✧ **Show up on the days and time you're expected.** Simple, yes? This may seem a small thing, but people not showing up—or showing up late—is perhaps the number one problem that organizations have with volunteers. They have a lot of work to do, and many schedules to coordinate. If they don't know who's going to show up and when, their job simply can't be done.

✧ **Call if you're going to miss your day or will be late.** This is more than just common courtesy. The volunteer organization relies on you, and if you give it fair notice, it will be able to figure out a way to cover for you while you're out.

✧ **Don't complain!** Count on it: There will be times when you're frustrated with your volunteer work. You'll notice that things aren't run perfectly. Perhaps people aren't there when they're supposed to be, or materials aren't ready. There are a thousand things that can go wrong in any organization, including volunteer organizations. But it does no good if you spend your time complaining. Accept that once in awhile things will go wrong. If you need to gripe, wait until you get home or are hanging out with your friends.

Helping Hands

After you sign on to do volunteer work, it's a good idea to get in writing exactly what will be expected of you. If the group doesn't put it in writing, do it yourself. Make a contract with yourself: Write down a series of promises relating to your volunteer experience and how you'll fulfill them. Sign and date the contract, and read it regularly to keep yourself on track.

✧ **Be helpful and courteous.** Maybe you had a rotten day at school, didn't get enough sleep last night, or your dad was on your case about cleaning your room for the ten-thousandth time. Once you get to your volunteering job, none of that matters. You need to be courteous and helpful, no matter what you're feeling.

✧ **Dress appropriately.** Leave the torn jeans, mini-skirts, and body jewelry at home, and cover up the tattoos. This is the real work world we're talking about, and none of that is appropriate.

✧ **Be enthusiastic.** When you volunteer, leave your too-cool-to-care look behind. Energy and enthusiasm are commodities that are in great demand. You have them in spades. Let them show!

✧ **Contribute new ideas.** When you volunteer, most groups will want more than just your time. They'll want your energy, your creativity, and your ideas as well. So don't merely follow orders. Think of ways things can be done better and how more people or animals can be helped. You'll be happier and you'll get more out of your experience that way. The group you volunteer for will be happier too. And the people or animals you're helping will reap the benefits.

✧ **Be yourself.** This final requirement may seem obvious, but it's not. It's easy to be frightened or put off by what's expected of you in a volunteer situation. And because of that, it can be difficult to let your real self shine through. But let it shine! The organization doesn't just want a warm body or a robot—they want you in all your glory! So be yourself. You'll be happier for it, and so will the organization. And most importantly, so will the people you're there to help.

How to Check Out an Organization Before Applying

You may not realize it, but you're a hot commodity! Volunteer organizations need your time, energy, and enthusiasm. That means you don't need to settle for a volunteer opportunity that isn't right for you. You can hold out for an ideal one.

But how do you know whether an organization is right for you? In the following sections, you'll find out how to check out that organization to make sure that it's a good one and matches what you need.

Information Station

If you're interested in volunteering for an organization, read the newspapers to see if there's any news about it—that will help you decide whether it's a good place to volunteer. And, in fact, newspapers are also great places to find out groups that might need volunteers.

Check the Basics

Let's start off with the most basic things you need to check out about an organization:

✧ **How big is the organization?** Is it part of a national group or a small local one? National groups often have more resources, but tend to be more bureaucratic. Smaller groups are often more open to new ideas, but may lack resources. Know what you're getting into before you volunteer, and find out the size of the organization.

✧ **How well-established is it?** New groups tend to be more disorganized, although they often have a higher energy level as well. Well-established groups are usually better organized, but at times can be a bit stodgy. There's nothing wrong with either kind of group, but before you volunteer, you should know what kind it will be.

Talk to the Members

When you go to an interview for the organization, you'll talk to one or possibly more than one person. During that interview, get as much information as you can. Ask how happy other volunteers have been. In particular, ask how many volunteers keep coming back. Also ask what kinds of things volunteers have gone on to do after they've volunteered at the organization.

Don't count on the single interview to provide you with all the information you want about the organization. Ask if you can talk to other people in the organization, especially people who you'll be working with directly. Sure, the president of the organization may seem great. But if the person you'll be working with has the personality of a serial killer, you won't be happy there.

Finally, don't be scared to ask difficult or awkward questions. If it looks to you as if the group is spending more money for nice offices than it spends helping others, ask where the money goes. If the group is a good one, it'll be happy to answer your question, and it'll respect you more for asking. If a group won't answer your question, you know it might not be worth spending your time with.

Helping Hands

Many organizations that use volunteers often have open meetings, such as board meetings, or just meetings of regular members. If you want to see what a group is really like before joining, attend one or more of those meetings. That'll give you a real look into what a group is like before you join.

Read the Newsletter or Visit the Web Site

An organization's newsletter or Web site is a look into its soul as well as its daily life. It will tell you about the group's activities, purpose, and give you a sense of how energetic the group is. So if possible, check out both the newsletter and the Web site before volunteering. In particular, look for these things:

✧ What is emphasized? The work the group does, or just the names of the leaders?

✧ Is there a calendar of upcoming events? If so, see whether these kinds of events are things you'd be interested in.

✧ Is there a list of goals and accomplishments? If so, check them out. They'll help you know whether the group is for you. If not, why aren't they there?

✧ Does it mention anything about volunteers? If so, what? Does it seem as if the newsletter or Web site emphasizes the importance of volunteers?

Information Station

Check the Internet for information about a group. There may be news stories, the group's home page, and discussions about the group. Using a search engine like www. yahoo.com or www.excite.com, type in the name of the group. You may find Web pages related to the group, including the group's home page, if it has one.

Ask About the Budget

If you're like most people, the very mention of the word "budget" sends shivers up and down your spine. No, not because it's an exciting topic. In fact, because of the opposite. Reading a budget is about as exciting as watching paint peel or the grass grow. Wake me when it's over!

But you'd be surprised at the amount of useful information buried in such a dull document. For example, you can find out whether the group is financially sound. You'll see what the group spends its money on—and so you'll know what the organization thinks is important. In short, you'll get a great advance peek of what the group thinks is important.

Talk to Other Volunteers

Let's say you've checked out an organization. You've found out the size of the group, and you know whether it's a new group or it's been around a while. You've talked to the members, you've asked the hard questions, you've examined the budget with a fine-tooth comb, and you've checked out the newsletter and Web site. So you think you have a pretty good idea of what the organization is like.

Think again.

There's one more thing you can do to check out the group—and in some ways, it's the most important thing. Talk to other volunteers, both current and past. They'll give you the best rundown you'll ever get on what it's like to volunteer there.

If you're meeting with current volunteers, talk to them at some place other than at the group's offices, since you may not get the most honest answer there. Get a phone number or e-mail address, or meet after school or after volunteering.

If you don't know how to get the names of other volunteers, just ask. A group will be more than happy to give you their names and contact information.

Inside Scoop

Teachers and guidance counselors can help you get the inside scoop on an organization. They may have had other students who have volunteered for the group, so they often have a very good sense of what the organization is like and what you can expect to get out of it.

The Least You Need to Know

✧ Among the things you may do as a volunteer are office work, fund-raising, newsletter writing, public relations, or hands-on work. Decide which you want to do before agreeing to volunteer.

✧ One of the biggest problems that organizations have is that volunteers burn out and stop showing up for work. Carefully plan your schedule to make sure you'll be able to do everything you promise for the organization.

✧ It's important that you show up on time and on schedule, that you be courteous and helpful, and that you dress appropriately for the job.

✧ Check out a group before agreeing to volunteer. Read its newsletter, visit its Web site, and check out its budget.

✧ Before volunteering, ask other volunteers what their experiences have been like with the group.

Chapter 4

Getting Your Dream Volunteering Job

In This Chapter

✧ What you need to know before you make your first contact with an organization

✧ Tracking down contact information for a group

✧ Tips for writing the perfect resumé

✧ How to prepare for an interview

✧ Conducting the perfect interview—and what to do afterwards

If you've followed the advice so far in this book, by now you've learned how to research and find an organization for which you want to volunteer. Now what? How to you go about getting that great volunteer job?

In this chapter, you'll learn the best way to contact an organization when you want to volunteer, you'll see how to write a resumé, and you'll find out how to conduct the perfect interview.

Getting in Touch with the Organization

You've decided on the kind of volunteering you want to do. Even better, you've decided on the organization for which you want to volunteer. Now it's time to get in touch.

How to Find the Group

Let's say that you're interested in volunteering for a group that helps clean the environment, called CleanIt Now! If you can't find contact information for the group, you can't get in touch with them. Start off by looking in your local Yellow Pages and White Pages. (Yellow Pages list businesses and organizations; White Pages list individuals and often businesses and organizations as well.) If the group is listed, you're in luck: Just copy down the phone number and address and you're ready. If this groups is not listed try calling Directory Assistance for the number.

If you have access to the Internet, head to www.superpages. com. It lets you search the entire country for businesses and organizations. Also, go to a big search engine like www. yahoo.com, www.lycos.com, or www.excite.com and type in the name of the place where you want to volunteer. You'll find many Web sites related to the group, including the group's home page, if it has one. In fact, there's often an even easier way to find the group's home page. Simply type in the group's name, surrounded by www. and .com, like this: www.cleanitnow.com.

Your school is a great place to start as well. There's a good chance your guidance counselor has contact information, and if not, he or she can get information for you. A personal contact is best—the name of someone. So get that if you can.

Making First Contact

Now you're ready to get in touch. When you make contact, you want to do three things:

1. Find out if there are any volunteer jobs available.

2. Find out who's in charge of coordinating volunteers.

3. Set up an interview.

The fastest way to get in touch is to make a phone call. If the thought of speaking with someone you don't know makes you nervous, I'd suggest having a little cheat sheet next to the telephone. Write down all the things you want to find out and all the things you want to say. That way, if you find yourself tongue-tied, you can always refer to it.

Information Station

An effective way to get in touch with a group is via e-mail. You'll find the e-mail address on the group's Web site or in its newsletter. To make sure you get through, you might follow up the e-mail with a phone call or via the regular mail.

Keep in mind that the receptionist may not have the best information, so ask who is in charge of volunteers. Then talk to that person. Leave a message if the person isn't in. If after a day or two you don't get a call back, call again. Don't worry, you're not being pushy. People at nonprofit groups or who accept volunteers are usually very busy and don't always return phone calls. So keep calling until you get the information you need.

When you talk to the person in charge of volunteering, explain the reasons why you want to volunteer. (Again, if you need to, keep a sheet of paper with this information nearby so that you can refer to it.) Then set up a time for an interview. Now you're on the road to a great volunteering experience!

Put Your Best Foot Forward: Writing a Resumé

Before you go to an interview, you should write a resumé. Don't start trembling—as I'll show you in this section, it's not as hard as you think. A resumé is really just a way for the organization to know more about you—what you're like and what you've done. I know, you're a teen, and you may think you haven't done a lot, but you've actually done a lot more than you might think.

What Is a Resumé, Anyway?

Let's start at the beginning. What exactly is a resumé? It's really nothing fancy. It's a summary of what you've done so far in your life, where you go to school, and your interests and accomplishments. For example, you might include being on a sports team, taking ballet lessons, or tutoring other kids.

Inside Scoop

A letter of recommendation will help you get a volunteer job. It's written by someone you know, and it extols all your virtues. Consider asking your guidance counselor or a teacher for one, but don't stop there. If you participate in any extracurricular activities, ask your coach or leader.

Your resumé should be short and to the point. A one-page resumé is best, but if you've done so much in your life that it can't fit on one page, then go ahead and stretch it to two.

What's in a Resumé?

What you'll put in a resumé is pretty straightforward. Here's what to include:

✧ **Your name, address, age, and contact information.** Contact information should include a telephone number. If you have an e-mail address and Web site, list them as well.

✧ **The school you attend.** If you take any special classes, such as Advanced Placement (AP) courses, list them. If you have a high average or grade point average (GPA) above a 3.0, list that as well.

✧ **Your objective in wanting the volunteer job.** Write a paragraph about why you want to volunteer. Be specific; don't merely say vague things like "I want to help people." Detail exactly why this particular opportunity is one that you want. For example, if you're trying to get a volunteer job at a daycare center, you might say that you're considering a career in teaching and this will give you a head start on your career.

✧ **Honors and awards.** Are you on the honor roll? Have you won any awards or received any special recognition? If so, list them all.

✧ **Any related experience.** If you've done any work or taken any classes related to the volunteer job, list that.

✧ **References.** List anyone who will agree to be a reference for you. Make sure to first ask the reference if it's okay to list him or her.

Tips for Resumé Writing

You know what should be in your resumé and what it should look like, so you're almost home. But if you want to write a great resumé, follow these tips:

✧ **Use active words.** Action words convey energy and a sense of dynamism, so whenever possible, use active verbs. For example, don't write "I was the person who had most of the fund-raising ideas." Instead, write "I spearheaded the fund-raising efforts."

✧ **Ask a teacher or parent to read it.** Teachers and parents may have a better sense of grammar than you do, so run it by them. And your parents have probably written or seen many resumés, so they might have some good tips for you.

✧ **Before you start, write about yourself on a blank sheet of paper.** List things you've done, why you're interested in the volunteer job, and anything else applicable. Feel free to ramble—the page is just for your reference. Once you have several paragraphs written about yourself, you're ready to write your resumé.

It's the Pits

One of the worst things you can do in a resumé is misspell a word (especially if you're volunteering to be a tutor!) Before printing out your resumé, check it carefully for spelling or grammatical errors (use the spell-check feature, too). Ask a friend, sibling, or parent to check it for errors as well.

What You Need to Know About Interviewing

So the big day is here. You've found the perfect volunteering opportunity, you've prepared a resumé, and you're ready for the interview. Don't panic! Interviews don't have to be stressful. Follow this advice, and you'll ace that interview!

It's Just Like the Scout Motto: Be Prepared

The simplest thing you can do to make sure that your interview goes well is be prepared. That's it. Spend a little time before the interview preparing, and you're sure to do well. Here's what you need to do:

✧ **Read up on the organization.** As outlined in Chapter 3, "Preparing for Your Volunteering Experience," read its newsletter, check the newspaper, and check the Web. If you show the interviewer that you know a great deal about the group, you'll impress him or her. And you'll be more likely to get the volunteering job.

Helping Hands

Make sure you know how to get to the organization before you go to an interview. Call ahead of time and get the directions. You might even want to make a trial run to the place to make sure you know how to get there.

✧ **Put together a list of things you'd like to accomplish.** List at least five. Type them up neatly and bring them with you. Whether or not the interviewer agrees with those things isn't the point. The point is that you've already taken the time to think about the opportunity and put something of yourself into it.

✧ **Prepare a list of questions you'd like to ask.** There's probably a lot you'd like to learn about the group. The

interview is the best chance you'll get to have those
questions answered.

✧ **Relax!** Easy to say, I know. But the more you relax before your interview, the better off you'll be.

How to Handle the Interview

Finally, time to head to the interview. Follow these tips and
you won't go wrong:

✧ **Show up on time.** The worst way to start an interview
is to show up late. It shows disrespect for the person
interviewing you, and it implies you don't care enough
about the opportunity to be on time.

✧ **Don't show up too early.** Showing up five minutes
ahead of time is fine. Showing up a half-hour early
isn't. So if you do get to the interview early, head to a
nearby coffee shop or take a walk around the block.

✧ **Be yourself.** You have nothing to hide, so just be who
you really are. If you try to be someone else, it'll show
and make you and the interviewer uncomfortable. And
if the interviewer doesn't like who you are, it's his or
her loss, after all, isn't it?

✧ **Dress appropriately.** No body piercings, no miniskirts
and fishnet stockings, no torn T-shirts and jeans ... you
get the idea. Dress nicely, and observe the usual habits
of good hygiene (that means not overdoing it with the
perfume or aftershave).

✧ **Answer questions clearly and directly.** Speak up so
you can be heard; answer confidently. If you don't understand a question, feel free to ask for clarification.

✧ **Ask questions.** Asking questions shows the interviewer
that you're engaged in the interview and that you care
about the group. Also, remember that you're interviewing the organization as much as it's interviewing you.

After all, you only want to volunteer if the group is a good match.

✧ **Present the things you'd like to accomplish.** Before the interview, you prepared a list. Hand it over and talk about it.

✧ **Watch your body language.** Your body language says a lot about you to others. Sit up straight. Look the interviewer in the eye; if you avoid eye contact you'll seem shady and untrustworthy. Don't appear sullen or bored; let your enthusiasm shine through.

Information Station

To learn more on interviewing and writing your resumé, check out *The Complete Idiot's Guide to the Perfect Interview*, by Marc Dorio (Alpha Books, 1997) and *The Complete Idiot's Guide to the Perfect Resume*, 2nd Edition, by Susan Ireland (Alpha Books, 2000). Both are packed with helpful tips.

What to Do After the Interview

When the interview ends, shake hands with the interviewer. Sometimes at the end of the interview, you'll be told that the volunteer job is yours. If this happens, you're in—just get the details of when to show up and how to prepare and you're ready to go.

Often, though, you may be told that you'll be informed about the next step at some later time. If you're told that, you don't have to simply wait. There are things you can do to follow up after the interview which may help you get the opportunity.

Ask the interviewer if you can follow up with a phone call or e-mail in a few days. It's always a good idea to send the interviewer an e-mail or letter after the interview, thanking him or her for interviewing you and reiterating your interest in the volunteer job. Then several days later, call or e-mail to follow up. Don't be a pest, but do make the contact—it will show you're serious and interested.

The Least You Need to Know

✧ Check the Yellow Pages, the Internet, directory assistance, and school guidance counselors if you don't know how to get in touch with a group.

✧ When you first make contact, find out if there are any volunteer jobs available, find out who's in charge of co-ordinating volunteers, and set up an interview.

✧ When you write a resumé, include all of your contact information, why you want to volunteer, and any awards, recognition, or related experience you have.

✧ Spell-check your resumé, and have someone else check it for clarity and proper grammar.

✧ Before your interview, put together a list of five things you'd like to accomplish at the organization, and talk about these goals during the interview.

✧ Show up on time for your interview, dress appropriately, be direct, ask questions, and be yourself.

Part 3
Finding Volunteering Experiences

It's time to volunteer! In this part, you'll get a complete guide to every volunteer opportunity you can imagine, and then some. You'll find out about volunteering in hospitals, nursing homes, and other health institutions; for the needy; at zoos and animal shelters; helping the environment; building better neighborhoods; for the arts; in politics and government; for literacy and education; and for police and fire departments as well as emergency medical services.

For every kind of volunteering, you'll get an inside look at what kinds of things you'll do. I'll tell you about any special issues you need to consider and how you can find a place to volunteer near you. You'll also get comprehensive volunteer resource guides.

Chapter 5

Volunteering in Hospitals and Health Organizations

In This Chapter

✧ Finding out about the different kinds of health-related volunteering you can do

✧ How to decide whether health-related volunteering is for you

✧ Special issues to be aware of before doing health-related volunteering

✧ Finding a health-related volunteering opportunity near you

✧ The medical volunteers resource guide

One of the most satisfying—and demanding—kinds of volunteer work you can do is to volunteer in hospitals and other health institutions and organizations. You'll help people at the most vulnerable time of their lives. The hours you spend every week pay for themselves many times over in the difference you can make in people's lives.

Even if you don't work directly with people in a hospital, there's still a lot you can do. You can help in fund-raising, blood drives, public awareness programs, and much more.

In this chapter, you'll learn about the kinds of volunteer work you can do in the health-related field, find out about any special requirements and get the rundown on how to find a volunteer opportunity in your town. So what are you waiting for? There are people who need your help—and you'll find that the hours you spend helping them may be the most satisfying hours that you'll ever spend.

What Kind of Work Will You Do?

If you're interested in volunteering to help people in hospitals, nursing homes, and other health institutions, you'll find a wide variety of things you can do. More than almost any other kind of volunteer work, it runs the full gamut of experiences—from directly helping patients to helping the medical staff, to aiding with fund-raising, to offering help to family members of the ill, and even to working with medical researchers.

There are many different kinds of health institutions that need your help: hospitals, public health departments other health institutions, and local branches of national health organizations such as the March of Dimes.

In this section, you'll learn about all the places you can volunteer and the kinds of work you can do at each. (To learn about volunteering in nursing homes, turn to Chapter 6, "Helping the Elderly and Caring for the Needy.")

Working in Hospitals

Hospitals always need volunteers, and so most hospitals have well-established volunteer programs. In general, there are three kinds of things you'll do in hospitals: working with patients, working with the hospital staff, and working with the public.

Working with Patients

If you love working directly with people and helping them, this kind of work is perfect for you. You'll work with the nursing and hospital staff to help patients in many different ways:

✧ **Escort patients around the hospital.** If you've been to a hospital, especially a large, big-city one, you know what a confounding and confusing place it can be. There are labs, different testing centers, rehabilitation areas, and many other sections, sometimes spread out over many buildings in a rambling complex. Because of that, it's often very difficult for patients to get from one place to another. Volunteers can escort patients from area to area.

Helping Hands

For most people, the best part of a hospital stay is when they're better and can leave the hospital. As a volunteer, you may well be part of the happiest day in a patient's stay. There are few things more satisfying in health care— and you'll be amazed at the gratitude that many people will show you!

✧ **Bring books and magazines.** In some hospitals, a library cart of books and magazines is brought around to the patients. Volunteers often bring this cart around.

✧ **Feed patients and make their beds.** Hospital patients need to eat three meals a day, which means thousands and thousands of meals delivered. Volunteers bring food to patients and sometimes feed them as well. Beds need to be made every day, so volunteers often do that also.

✧ **Help the nurses.** Nurses need all kinds of help. For example, you can help answer call lights to see what patients require, and then report back to the nurses. Sometimes, with a nurse's help, you'll be able to handle the patient's request yourself. And you may also get a chance to help nurses in recovery rooms who are caring for patients after surgery.

Helping Hands

You may not think you're doing a lot to help hospital patients, but just your presence there does a great deal to lift their spirits. Knowing that someone cares enough to volunteer is a great boost—especially when that volunteer is young, helpful, and energetic.

✧ **Help with physical therapy.** Some patients have to go through physical therapy in order to recuperate from an illness or surgery; for example, after knee surgery. You can be part of a patient's physical therapy by doing things like helping the patient learn how to use crutches.

Working with Staff

There are many behind-the-scenes things that need to be done at hospitals, most notably helping the staff. While this may not seem to directly help the patients, in fact it does. Because if you can free the staff from chores and help with other chores, they can spend more time with patients. Working with staff is great for someone who wants to help in a hospital, but doesn't feel comfortable working directly with patients. Here are some of the things you can do to help staff:

✧ **File and work with medical records.** Hospitals produce paperwork in enormous amounts. They need help filing records and handling all kinds of paperwork.

✧ **Be a messenger and handle supplies.** Requests, records, supplies, and paperwork need to be delivered throughout the hospital. You can help do all that.

✧ **Answer telephones.** Telephones ring all day long at a hospital. You can help by answering phones and routing the calls to the proper people. And you can answer certain questions yourself, such as giving directions to the hospital.

It's the Pits

Some of the things you do in a hospital, such as feeding patients, may seem very difficult to do. Don't worry—you won't be left on your own. If you volunteer in a hospital you'll get training to do anything that you're asked.

Working with the Public

A hospital is teeming with patients, family members, and visitors. Hospital staff can easily become overwhelmed with helping them. Here's what you can do when you volunteer:

✧ **Work at the gift shop.** Hospital gift shops always need help. You can work as a sales clerk and help people choose gifts for patients.

✧ **Work at the information desk.** People coming into a
hospital have all kinds of questions—usually about
where to find a certain room or doctor. You can give
them directions.

✧ **Work at the cafeteria or coffee shop.** You can help
serve the food, take orders, work the cash registers, and
help clean up.

Working in a Health Department

Local, state, and national governments all have health departments of various kinds. And often, they need help. Health departments make sure that the water we drink doesn't cause
disease. They inspect food-packaging plants and restaurants.
They run public awareness programs about things such as
breast cancer, the dangers of tobacco, the importance of im-
munization, and using safety belts for children. They immu-
nize children as well as adults and generally work to control
the spread of disease. Help is especially needed in the fall and
early winter, when health departments run flu shot clinics.

Inside Scoop

One way health departments combat teen smoking is by
making sure no stores sell cigarettes to teens. The health
departments conduct "sting" operations—they use teen
volunteers.

Here are the kinds of things you might do when volunteering
for a health department:

✧ **Help with educational programs.** Health departments
need people to help write and distribute educational

materials, and to help educate the public about a variety of health problems.

✧ **Help with flu clinics.** Long lines can form at public health clinics that give flu shots during the fall and early winter. Volunteers help with registration, setting up appointments, and more.

✧ **Do office work.** Using the computer, filing, answering telephones ... public health departments sometimes use volunteers for this kind of work.

Volunteering for Other Health Organizations

There are many other kinds of health organizations that need volunteers, most notably organizations like the March of Dimes, which helps fight birth defects. Often, you'll volunteer at the local branches of national organizations.

Because these organizations are so varied, the kinds of work you'll do for them is amazingly varied as well. There's no way to cover the full gamut of what you'll do, but here's a short list:

✧ **Help with blood drives.** Many organizations help the Red Cross with blood drives. Blood is needed so that when people need transfusions in hospitals, there's always an adequate supply. You can, of course, give blood. But you can also help organize and run blood drives.

✧ **Help with fund-raising.** One of the most common ways of helping a national health organization is to help with fund-raising. This can mean helping organize and participate in walk-a-thons and phone-a-thons as well as many other kinds of fund-raising activities.

✧ **Do office work.** You can answer the telephones, file, use computers, and do the thousand-and-one things that always need doing at nonprofit organizations.

✧ **Help with publicity.** Nonprofit health organizations always need publicity for things like fund-raising or to help educate the public about a health matter.

Inside Scoop

The March of Dimes has one of the most comprehensive teen volunteer programs in the country. At the heart of their volunteer work is the Chain Reaction Youth Leadership Program. Volunteers organize major events such as the WalkAmerica walk-a-thon, as well as smaller events such as volleyball tournaments, dances, car washes, and carnivals.

Is Volunteering in Health Care for You?

To help you decide whether this field is for you, I'll go over the pros and cons of volunteering for health care. After reviewing each section, you'll be much further along in deciding whether it's right for you.

The Pros of Volunteering in Health Care

There are many reasons why volunteering in health care is a great idea. Here are the most important ones:

✧ **There's no greater satisfaction than helping those who are ill.** You'll see an immediate impact to your volunteering—something that you won't get in many other kinds of volunteer work. And you'll be helping people at what is often the most difficult time of their lives.

✧ **You'll form strong bonds with people.** When you care for someone who's ill, or work with people who care for others, you tend to form very strong bonds with them— relationships that are difficult to form any other way.

✧ **You'll often be recognized.** Since the volunteering work is so demanding, those who volunteer in health often gain recognition of some sort—not only from the people you're directly helping, but among the health care staff as well.

✧ **It's a great way to find out whether you want a career in health care.** Careers in health care are often very demanding. If you volunteer now, it will give you a good sense of whether it's something you want to devote your life to.

Inside Scoop

Before you can volunteer in a hospital or similar health institution, your doctor may have to fill out a medical form about your health. This kind of volunteering can be physically demanding, and the institution will want to make sure that you're healthy enough to fulfill your responsibilities.

The Cons of Volunteering in Health Care

Volunteering in health care isn't for everyone. It's one of the most demanding (and for many people, one of the most satisfying) types of volunteer work you can do. Here are some of the cons:

✧ **It's very demanding.** You may find yourself volunteering many hours a week, which could be too much for your schedule.

✧ **It can be high-stress.** You may feel a great deal of pressure volunteering for health care, especially if you care for people directly. Take that into account before deciding whether it's for you.

✧ **You may have to face difficult issues.** For some people, it's difficult and unpleasant to work with people who are ill. If you'll be working directly with ill people, make sure you can handle it.

Special Issues with Health Care Volunteering

In some ways, health care volunteering is different than any other type of volunteering. Especially if you work directly with ill people or handle ay medical records, there are some special issues you need to be aware of.

First, you should realize that there may be age requirements when it comes to certain kinds of volunteering. Some hospitals may not allow you to volunteer if you're under 17 years old. So check with hospitals to see if there are age limits.

Other kinds of health volunteering may have similar age requirements. For example, you may need to be a certain age before you can volunteer to help at flu shot clinics. In fact, you may also need to be a certain age even to help with filing in a hospital or health facility. And there are other issues connected with medical records as well. They are supposed to be kept private, and if you are able to work with them, you'll be subject to very strict privacy requirements. That means you're not allowed to talk to anyone about the information found in them.

There are other kinds of special requirements that you should keep in mind. This kind of volunteering can be very physically demanding. For example, you may have to wheel people around a hospital in a wheelchair, or lift them in and out of a wheelchair, which can become tiring very quickly. Or you may have to move medical supplies, which is physically demanding as well.

Also keep in mind that if you do volunteer in a health institution, it's much more important that you show up, and show up on time. If you're directly helping people, they'll be relying on you. It's a commitment that you can't take lightly.

Finally, be aware that volunteering to help in health institutions requires strong people skills—you must enjoy working with other people and be able to get along with others. That doesn't mean that you can't volunteer in a health institution if you're shy—it just means that you might consider volunteering for a job where you don't have to work directly with people. For example, you might want to file records instead.

Information Station

A great resource for finding a place to volunteer in health care is with your family or at your place of worship. Your parents will know the names of nearby hospitals, health institutions, and health-related organizations. And your place of worship will have a comprehensive list of health-related organizations.

Finding a Place to Volunteer Near You

Let's say you've decided that volunteering in health care is for you. Now it's time to find a place to volunteer. How to do it? Hospitals and health organizations such as the March of Dimes rely greatly on volunteers, and so they have well-established volunteer programs. If you're interested in volunteering in a hospital, just check in the Yellow Pages and you'll find a list of all the nearby hospitals. Call the main number for the hospital and tell the receptionist you want to volunteer.

Information Station

Want a quick way to find a volunteer opportunity? Check your phone directory's Blue Pages, which lists government offices. Look for your town's health department, then give them a call. If you live near your state capital, call the state's health agency for help.

In fact, the best way to find out about volunteer opportunities for health-related organizations in general is by checking your Yellow Pages. Look under listings such as Hospitals, Health Clinics, Health Agencies, and Social Service Organizations. Also check the state and local government listings, which are often in the Blue Pages, a section of your local White Pages. Look for the Department of Public Health, Council on the Aging, Health Department, and similar listings. It's also a good idea to call your town or city hall, and explain that you want to volunteer for a health organization. You'll be put through to the department that can help you.

Another good place to check is your family physician. He or she is hooked into the health care system and will know where to point you—and be more than happy to do it, as well. Libraries are also excellent places to check.

Medical Volunteers Resource Guide

There are many hundreds of places you can volunteer if you're interested in health-related volunteering. But if you're having trouble finding a place near you, don't worry—I've provided a resource guide for you to help. Here are some of the best organizations you'll find to put you in touch with a volunteer opportunity. I've listed the national headquarters of the organizations. Contact the headquarters and let them know you're looking for something in your area.

AIDS Action

This group is a network of 3,200 national AIDS service organizations. If you're looking to volunteer at an AIDS organization, it's a great place to start.

1906 Sunderland Place NW
Washington, D.C. 20036
www.aidsaction.org

American Cancer Society

This group is the main organization for leading the fight against cancer through fund-raising, public education, and lobbying the government.

1599 Clifton Road NE
Atlanta, GA 30329
1-800-ACS-2345 or 404-320-3333
www.cancer.org

American Council of the Blind

This group helps the blind in many ways, and has state and regional groups associated with it. It uses many volunteers and always needs help.

1155 15th Street NW
Suite 1004
Washington, D.C. 20005
1-800-424-8666 or 202-467-5081
www.acb.org

American Heart Association

This organization fights heart disease and stroke. It does a great deal of fund-raising and public education.

7272 Greenville Avenue
Dallas, TX 75231
214-373-6300
www.americanheart.org

American Lung Association

The American Lung Association works to prevent lung disease and promotes lung health.

1740 Broadway
New York, NY 10019
212-315-8700
www.lungusa.org

Information Station

If you're interested in promoting lung health and helping fight the killer disease tuberculosis in the U.S. as well as overseas, there are many places you can contact to see if they want volunteers. Go to www.iuatld.org/html/ body_ links.htm for a comprehensive list.

American Medical Association

The American Medical Association is the country's largest organization of doctors. It's a great clearinghouse for finding out any information about medicine, and so is helpful for finding volunteer opportunities.

515 North State Street
Chicago, IL 60610
312-464-5000
www.ama-assn.org

American Public Health Association

State public health associations do a great deal of public education and are good places to volunteer—or to find other places to volunteer.

800 I Street NW
Washington, D.C. 20001
202-777-APHA
www.apha.org

American Red Cross

The American Red Cross helps victims of disasters such as hurricanes, collects half the nation's blood supply through donations, and teaches cardiopulmonary resuscitation (CPR), among other jobs. It uses many, many volunteers in different ways.

431 18th Street NW
Washington, D.C. 20006
202-639-3520
www.redcross.org

Campaign for Tobacco-Free Kids

This group works to stamp out smoking among kids and teens. A lot of the work of the group is done by teen and kid volunteers.

1707 L Street NW
Suite 800
Washington, D.C. 20036
202-296-5469
www.tobaccofreekids.org

March of Dimes

The March of Dimes fights birth defects and has many different kinds of well-established volunteer organizations.

1275 Mamaroneck Avenue
White Plains, NY 10605
1-888-663-4637
www.modimes.org

Special Olympics

The Special Olympics provide sports training and athletic competition in a variety of Olympic-style sports for people with mental handicaps. The organization relies very heavily on volunteers.

1325 G Street NW
Suite 500
Washington, D.C. 20005
202-628-3630
www.specialolympics.org

The Least You Need to Know

✧ Hospitals are great places to volunteer because they have well-established volunteering programs.

✧ When you volunteer at a hospital, you may work directly with patients, help the medical staff, or help the public at places like an information desk.

✧ Public health departments and health organizations like the Red Cross and March of Dimes often need volunteers for fund-raising and public education efforts.

✧ Doing health-related volunteering can be satisfying, but if you work directly with patients, it can be very demanding, both physically and emotionally.

✧ In order to work in a hospital or some other health organizations, you may have to be over a certain age.

✧ To find a place to volunteer, check local hospitals, the Yellow Pages, your local health department, or ask your family doctor.

Chapter 6

Helping the Elderly and Caring for the Needy

In This Chapter

✧ The kinds of work you'll do when you volunteer to help the elderly

✧ What you can do to help the homeless

✧ Helping to feed the hungry

✧ How to decide whether volunteering to help the elderly or needy is for you

✧ How to find an organization near you that helps the elderly or needy

✧ Resource guide for those who want to volunteer to help the elderly or needy

Chances are there are seniors living near you who need help caring for themselves, or who would be grateful to have people help them handle day-to-day tasks. And there are countless people every day in this country and across the world who go hungry, or who are homeless.

In this chapter, you'll learn all about what it means to volunteer to help the elderly and the needy, and you'll find out how to find an organization that needs your help, right near where you live.

What Kind of Work Will You Do?

Volunteering to help the elderly, homeless, and hungry is some of the most satisfying work you can do. Much of this kind of work is one-on-one, which means that you'll see the results of your efforts, like the smile you get when you visit a newfound senior friend in a nursing home. You'll also get the satisfaction of knowing you've helped someone hungry get a square meal.

There are many different ways to help people. You can help the elderly in nursing homes, senior centers, and in their own homes. You can work in shelters and help families, the homeless, and battered women. And you can work for one of the many organizations that help feed the hungry, in places like soup kitchens, or help raise funds through things like walks against hunger.

In this section, you'll learn about all the places you can volunteer, and the kinds of work you can do at each.

Helping Hands

You don't need to join an organization in order to help the elderly—there are things you can do right in your own neighborhood. If you have an elderly neighbor, offer to shovel his or her sidewalk in the winter, clean the yard, or do any of many other kinds of physically demanding chores that are difficult when one ages.

Working with the Elderly

There are many ways you can help the elderly if you're interested in volunteering. It can be as simple as shoveling snow off a senior's driveway who is no longer capable of shoveling, or as regular as volunteering several days a week at a nursing home.

No matter what you do, however, you'll find that the elderly greatly appreciate your help. It's not just that they're being helped by someone—it's that a young person cares enough about them to donate his or her time.

Volunteering at a Nursing Home

Almost all nursing homes need volunteers. Generally, when you volunteer in a nursing home, you'll work directly with the elderly, but you can also work with the staff.

People in nursing homes are generally there because they can no longer care for themselves. Often they have medical problems or disabilities of some sort. When you volunteer in a nursing home, you'll help the same person or people each week and will develop a relationship with that person. And developing that relationship is helpful not only for the person you're helping, but for you as well. You'll find that the elderly often have a great deal of advice and wisdom they'll be willing to share, as well as some pretty amazing life stories.

Here are some of the things you can do when you volunteer in a nursing home:

- ✧ **Provide companionship.** This is probably the most important thing you can do for someone in a nursing home. All too often, the elderly feel as if they've been abandoned and forgotten by society—and in fact, they often have. Your friendship and companionship will do more for their lives than you can imagine.

- ✧ **Be an escort.** Some elderly are in wheelchairs or have to use walkers, and so have a good deal of difficulty getting around by themselves. You can push a wheelchair,

69

open doors, and generally help them to get from place to place.

✧ **Play games.** Yes, believe it or not, you can play games as a volunteer! Card games, board games, chess, checkers, games of any kind—they're all great fun and will provide an hour or two of entertainment not just for the senior, but for you as well.

Inside Scoop

I used to visit a senior in his home, more to keep him company than to do chores. I know that my visits meant a lot to him, but I think I got even more out of our friendship than he did. He had been in vaudeville when he was younger and had a remarkable life story—one I never would have heard if I hadn't spent time with him every week.

✧ **Read books and newspapers.** Some older people have a hard time seeing or may be seriously visually impaired. You can help out by reading newspapers and books to them. And if they have a difficult time writing, you can write letters for them as well.

✧ **Teach about computers.** Some nursing homes have computers and computer rooms—but sometimes the elderly aren't experienced enough to know how to use them. That's where you come in—you can teach them one-on-one how to click and surf.

✧ **Help the staff.** Nursing home staff always needs help. It can be office help, like filing, photocopying, and using a computer. Or you can answer the telephone, help with fund-raising, and numerous other tasks.

Helping Out at Home

Many seniors live at home but need help living independently, or need companionship for other reasons. Because of that, there are many volunteer opportunities if you want to help the elderly at home. Here are some of the things you can do:

✦ **Provide companionship.** The elderly at home often need companionship. They want someone to talk to, to befriend, to play games with. In short, they want to know that someone cares about them. You'll find it incredibly gratifying to provide this kind of companionship for an elderly person living alone at home.

✦ **Call by telephone to check in.** Some programs call the elderly every day just to check in and make sure that they're healthy and everything is okay. For example, the Burden Center for Aging in New York City has a program called Telefriend in which teen and adult volunteers call the elderly every day to check in and make sure things are fine.

Helping Hands

Senior centers are places where the elderly gather for classes, companionship, meals, and more. Very often, senior centers are looking for volunteers to help with classes (or even teach them), help make meals, and more.

✧ **Go food shopping.** To you, going food shopping is a simple task. However, to some elderly people it's a difficult, demanding chore. You can help people living at home by escorting them to the supermarket, or doing the grocery shopping for them.

✧ **Help Meals on Wheels.** Meals on Wheels is a program that delivers hot meals to the elderly in their homes. It often needs volunteers of many different kinds.

✧ **Do housework and cooking.** When someone is infirm, it's often difficult for them to do even the simplest kinds of housework. Many need help cooking, too.

✧ **Escort them when they're out of the house.** If someone is in a wheelchair, requires a walker, or has other difficulty getting around, an escort is a big help. You can push a wheelchair, help them as they do neighborhood errands, drive them to appointments, or just take a walk with them so they can get some fresh air.

Working in Shelters

It's a sad fact that today in the United States, the most affluent country in the world, many people are homeless, including families with children. There are other kinds of shelters as well—shelters for battered women and their children, if they have any. It's another sad fact that many women are beaten by the men in their lives, and in order to escape are forced to live in a shelter.

Working in Women's Shelters

You won't work directly with battered women at shelters, because it's a very difficult task, and only properly trained adults can do it. However, there are a number of ways you'll be able to help:

✧ **Raise funds.** Shelters rarely have enough money and always need more funds. So you can participate in fund-raising through fund drives, working in thrift shops that give their profits to the shelter, and in other ways.

✧ **Baby sit.** Many of the women in shelters have children with them, and so need baby sitters while they're being counseled or out working.

✧ **Help the shelter staff.** There's always a variety of tasks that the shelter staff needs help with, including clerical work and cleaning.

It's the Pits

Not all women's shelters want male volunteers. That can be disturbing to some women. So if you're a male, be aware that you may not be allowed to volunteer at a women's shelter.

Working in Shelters for the Homeless

Shelters for the homeless provide places for those without homes to sleep, to get food, and to get counseling. Shelters always need volunteers. Here are some of the main things you can do at a shelter for the homeless:

✧ **Raise funds.** Just like most other kinds of help organizations, shelters for the homeless need people to raise funds through fund drives and in other ways as well.

✧ **Serve food.** Many shelters also need volunteers to help feed the homeless. You can get the food ready for cooking by doing things such as washing vegetables, put together salads, help serve the food, and clean up.

✧ **Helping the staff.** Homeless shelters always have a wide variety of work that needs doing, from clerical work to cleanup.

Inside Scoop

If you want to help the homeless and the hungry, a great time to do so is on Thanksgiving. Homeless shelters need volunteers to raise funds, prepare and serve the food, clean up, and help in other ways. Thanksgiving is often a difficult time for the homeless and hungry, so it's a great time to volunteer.

Helping Feed the Hungry

Millions of people go hungry every day here in the United States and around the world. If you want to help feed the hungry, there are many different things you can do. You can work directly with people and serve food in a soup kitchen. Or you can help round up food for food banks. You can also help with fund-raising efforts. No matter what you do, you'll have the satisfaction of knowing that you're fighting one of the world's biggest problems.

Here are some of the ways you can help feed the hungry:

✧ **Work in a soup kitchen.** "Soup kitchen" is a general term used for any place that feeds the hungry. You can help in fund-raising, preparing and serving foods, and helping out the staff.

✧ **Help at a food bank and food drive.** Food drives and food banks stockpile nonperishable goods, such as canned foods and cereals, to help feed the hungry.

They need help getting the word out, gathering and storing the food, and delivering it as well. Food drives are frequently done during the Thanksgiving and Christmas seasons.

✧ **Helping national organizations.** Many organizations such as the Salvation Army and Oxfam America help feed the hungry. They have branches all over the country. These groups need help fund-raising, getting publicity, signing up members, and many more kinds of jobs as well.

Inside Scoop

My family and I have been volunteering to help feed the hungry for decades. When I was in high school, I helped organize a walk for hunger. As a teen, my younger brother Eliot devoted an enormous amount of time to volunteering to feed the hungry. My children have also participated in the annual Walk for Hunger in the Boston area.

Is Helping the Elderly or Needy for You?

There are many different opportunities open to you if you want to help the elderly or needy. But helping people in this way isn't for everyone. To help you decide, I'll go over the pros and cons.

The Pros of Volunteering for the Elderly or Needy

There are many reasons why volunteering to help the elderly

or needy is a great idea. Here are the most important ones:

✧ **You'll see an immediate difference in people's lives.** Many of the elderly need a great deal of help and are enormously appreciative of what you do for them.

✧ **You'll get a sense of satisfaction.** Few needs are as immediate as hunger. You'll know that the work you're doing is vitally important.

✧ **You'll save children's lives.** Some of the groups that you can work for, such as Oxfam, raise money to help feed children dying of hunger in other parts of the world.

✧ **You can volunteer only when you want to or when your schedule permits.** If you want to help the hungry, for example, you can volunteer to work on a food drive instead of volunteering every week.

✧ **You'll form strong bonds with people.** When you care for the elderly, you tend to form very strong bonds—relationships that are difficult to form any other way.

The Cons of Volunteering for the Elderly or Needy

Volunteering for the elderly or needy isn't for everyone. It's often very demanding, and because you may come face to face with people who have fallen on hard times, it can be emotionally wrenching as well. Here are some cons to consider:

✧ **It can be emotionally demanding.** While it's incredibly satisfying to help people in these kinds of difficulties, it can be draining as well. People who are homeless may have mental health problems, for example. Seniors may be in bad health. In short, it can be strong stuff.

✧ **It can be high-stress.** You may feel a great deal of pressure volunteering for health care, especially if you care for people directly.

Special Issues with Helping the Elderly or Needy

There are some things you should realize before you volunteer to help the elderly or needy. First, in many instances you may not be able to help the needy directly. At homeless shelters or shelters for battered women, for example, your contact may be limited to doing things such as serving food. That's because it's best for trained professionals to work directly with people who are facing difficult life problems.

Some places may also have a minimum age limit on volunteering, so make sure to double-check any place you want to volunteer.

It's the Pits

Our society doesn't always portray the elderly in a positive light. On television the elderly are often the object of demeaning jokes or portrayed in sometimes ludicrously stereotypical ways. Because of that, some people—including some teens—belittle the elderly. Make sure you won't demean or make fun of them while you're helping them.

Finding a Place to Volunteer Near You

Let's say you've decided that volunteering for the elderly or needy is for you. Now it's time to find a place to volunteer. How to do it? As you'll see in this section, most organizations that help the elderly or needy actively seek out volunteers, and have well-established programs for getting and training volunteers. If you're interested in volunteering at a nursing home or senior center, just check in the Yellow Pages and you'll find a list of nursing homes and senior centers in your area. Call the main numbers and tell the receptionist you want to volunteer.

Also check the state and local government listings, which are often in the Blue Pages, a section of your local White Pages. Look for the Department of Human Services, Council on the Aging, Health Department, and similar listings. It's also a good idea to call your town or city hall, and explain that you want to volunteer for the hungry. You'll be put through to the department that can help you.

Libraries are also excellent places to check. Go to the reference desk. There's nothing librarians like more than tracking down information for people. They do it for a living, so they're good at it, too. Also check with churches, synagogues, and other places of worship. They usually have very strong programs helping the elderly or needy. You might ask your parents, teachers, or guidance counselors as well.

Information Station

How's this for a simple way to find a place to volunteer: Check with your grandparents, great-aunts, great-uncles, or other elderly relatives. If they live near you, ask them about senior centers and similar organizations that might need volunteers. They'll no doubt have many ideas right at hand.

Resource Guide for Volunteering for the Elderly or Needy

There are many hundreds of places you can volunteer if you're interested in volunteering for the elderly or needy.

But if you're having trouble finding a place near you, don't worry—I've provided a resource guide for you to help. Here are some of the best organizations you'll find to put you in touch with a volunteer opportunity. I've listed the national headquarters of the organizations. Contact the headquarters and let them know you're looking for something in your area.

Alliance for Families and Children

The Alliance for Families and Children is made up of 350 organizations that help children and families. It helps over five million people in more than 2,000 communities, so it's a great place for finding volunteer experiences for helping the needy.

11700 W. Lake Park Drive
Milwaukee, WI 53224
1-800-221-3726
www.alliance1.org

American Association of Retired People (AARP)

The AARP is the country's largest organization for people 50 years old and older. It's also a great place to turn to find out about volunteering for seniors.

601 E Street NW
Washington, D.C. 20049
1-800-424-3410
www.aarp.org

American Red Cross

The American Red Cross helps provide shelter for people who have been victims of disasters such as hurricanes.

431 18th Street NW
Washington, D.C. 20006
202-639-3520
www.redcross.org

Inside Scoop

When you think of the homeless, you may picture beggars who are single men. But that's far from the truth, according to studies done by the U.S. Conference of Mayors. Studies found that 38 percent of the homeless population were in fact families, and that children under 18 make up 25 percent of the urban homeless.

Meals on Wheels Association of America

Meals on Wheels are local organizations that deliver hot meals to seniors across the country. Check the national headquarters to find a branch near you.

1-800-677-1116
www.projectmeal.org

National Coalition for the Homeless

The National Coalition for the Homeless is devoted to helping the homeless in a variety of ways. It's a great place to find out how you can volunteer to help homeless people.

1012 14th Street NW
Suite 600
Washington, D.C. 20005
202-737-6444
http://nch.ari.net

National Council on the Aging

The National Council on the Aging is devoted to helping seniors in many different ways. It's an excellent resource for finding out how to volunteer to help the elderly.

409 Third Street SW
Washington, D.C. 20024
Phone 202-479-1200
www.ncoa.org

Oxfam America

Oxfam America helps fight hunger, poverty, and social injustice throughout the world. It's particularly active in helping fight hunger and feed the hungry.

26 West Street
Boston, MA 02111
1-800-77OXFAM or 617-482-1211
www.oxfamamerica.org

The Salvation Army

The Salvation Army helps people in many ways, notably by feeding the hungry and providing shelters for the homeless.

1025 F Street NE
Washington, D.C. 20002
202-783-0233
www.salvationarmy.org

United Way of America

United Ways are local organizations across the country that help the needy, seniors, the hungry, and the homeless in many different ways.

701 North Fairfax Street
Alexandria, VA 22314
703-836-7112
www.unitedway.org

The Least You Need to Know

✧ If you're interested in helping the elderly, you can volunteer in a nursing home, a senior center, or right at the home of a senior.

✧ Some of the most common ways to volunteer to help the elderly are by escorting them; helping them with housework, shopping, and cooking; and being a companion.

✧ When you volunteer in a nursing home, you'll often help the same person or people every week.

✧ Shelters for the homeless need people to raise funds and to help prepare and serve food.

✧ You can help feed the hungry by participating in food drives—and you can do it just at a particular time of year if you want, not year-round.

Chapter 7

Volunteering at Zoos and Animal Shelters

In This Chapter

✧ The kinds of work you can do when you volunteer to help animals

✧ The different kinds of places where you can volunteer to help animals

✧ What you need to know about volunteering in zoos and aquariums

✧ What you need to know about volunteering in shelters, pounds and in animal hospitals

✧ How to decide if you want to volunteer to help animals

✧ Complete resource guide for volunteering for animals

There are abandoned animals in shelters that need love and care, animals in zoos and aquariums that need looking after, and animals in animal hospitals that need your help.

If you're interested in volunteering to work with animals, there are many ways to help. So read on and find out everything there is to know about it.

What Kind of Work Will You Do?

There are many different kinds of places you can volunteer if you want to work with animals. You can volunteer at zoos, animal shelters, and animal hospitals. And there are many different kinds of jobs you'll be able to do as well—everything from caring for abandoned animals, to cleaning up, to helping veterinarians, to helping raise funds, to making the public aware of the problems that face animals.

There are many well-established programs for volunteers who want to help animals, so it'll be easy to find a place. That's because many groups that help animals have budget problems and rely heavily on volunteers.

Where You'll Be Able to Volunteer

While there are many different kinds of places you can volunteer, there are three main ones: zoos and aquariums, shelters and pounds, and animal hospitals and veterinarian offices. Here's what you need to know about each.

It's the Pits

Depending on where you volunteer and what you do, there may be an age limit on working with animals. You may need to be 15 years or older, for example, if you want to work directly with animals, instead of just helping the staff. Find out before you agree to volunteer.

Volunteering at Zoos and Aquariums

Usually, zoos and aquariums are nonprofit groups, and so rely heavily on volunteers. Keep in mind that when you volunteer at a zoo or aquarium, you won't be working with pets—you'll be working with wild animals. Don't worry, that doesn't mean you're going to have to feed the lions. But it does mean that you'll often have less hands-on work with the animals than you would if you worked in a pound or animal shelter.

There are many different tasks you'll do at a zoo or aquarium. Here are some of the most common:

✧ **Give tours.** Young children and school groups often take tours of zoos and aquariums. As a tour guide you can show them around and answer questions.

✧ **Help feed and care for the animals.** No, you won't be put in a cage with a tiger, or expected to feed the polar bears. But you can help care for and feed some of the tamer, smaller animals, including rabbits, ferrets, and snakes. Only professionals will be allowed to feed the larger or more dangerous animals, though.

✧ **Help with maintenance.** There are always a thousand small tasks that need doing in zoos and aquariums. At aquariums, for example, you may need to regularly check the pH level of the water. You may also clean the places where animals are housed—not a pleasant task, but a very necessary and important one.

✧ **Track animal behavior.** Many zoos and aquariums do research on animals as well as care for them. You may be asked to take notes on animal behavior as part of this research or as part of their daily care.

✧ **Work in the gift store.** Many zoos and aquariums have gift stores that are often staffed by volunteers.

✧ **Raise funds.** Many zoos and aquariums are strapped for cash and must regularly do fund-raising. You can help by participating in fund drives.

✧ **Educate the public.** Part of the what zoos and aquariums do is educate the public about issues facing animals and wildlife. You can work on public education programs by helping to write, produce, and distribute newsletters and brochures.

Volunteering in Shelters and Pounds

Animal shelters and pounds are often desperate for volunteers, since many shelters in particular are largely staffed by volunteers.

Sadly, millions of animals end up at pounds and shelters across the country for a variety of reasons. A common reason is that they're strays—they don't belong to anyone. Animals also end up there if their owners don't want them any more, or if they've been taken away from their former owners because of abuse. If you're going to work in a shelter or pound, you may receive special training on working with abused animals and regaining their trust.

Inside Scoop

What's the difference between a pound and a shelter? Generally, a pound is run by a government agency, such as a town pound. Animal shelters, on the other hand, are usually run by nonprofit groups, such as the Society for the Prevention of Cruelty to Animals.

Many shelters are run by humane societies and groups such as the Society for the Prevention of Cruelty to Animals. These humane societies and groups do more than just take care of animals in shelters. They also reach out to the community to teach people about issues such as the problem of abused animals or the importance of spaying or neutering pets.

It's the Pits

If you work directly with animals at a shelter or pound, you may be required to get a rabies vaccination for your own protection. If you don't get the vaccination, you may not be allowed to work directly with the animals.

What you can do will vary from pound to pound and shelter to shelter. But in general, these are the kinds of things that you'll do:

✧ **Help the animals.** At some pounds and shelters, you'll work directly with the animals by caring for them, taking them for walks, feeding them, grooming them, and playing with them. You'll probably also help clean out the cages—not always a pleasant task, but one that desperately needs to be done.

✧ **Work in the foster care program.** Some shelters run foster care programs in which animals are placed in temporary homes. They might be placed in a temporary home to recover after an operation, or until a permanent owner can be found.

✧ **Help with maintenance, landscaping, and other chores.** Pounds and shelters always need all kinds of work like this done—and they are more than happy to have volunteers help them.

✧ **Work with the public.** Shelters, pounds, and humane societies work a great deal with the public. They need people to answer the telephones, to give people information about animals and shelters, and many other jobs.

✧ **Raise funds.** Most humane societies are nonprofit organizations that are always in need of money. They often have many fund-raising efforts, and always need volunteers to help in many different ways.

✧ **Become involved in lobbying campaigns.** Often, humane societies and similar organizations become involved in issues related to animal welfare. They may want to let people know about whether laboratory animals are treated well or abused, or they may try to get laws passed that have to do with animal welfare. They always need volunteers to help in lobbying and in political campaigns.

Helping Hands

The Massachusetts Society for the Prevention of Cruelty to Animals has a unique volunteer program that allows volunteers to help the elderly. In the society's pet visitation program, people bring their pets to senior centers or nursing homes. The residents of the home or center get a chance to spend time with your pet. It's a great way for you to help others while sharing your special pet with the world.

Volunteering in Animal Hospitals and Veterinarian Offices

Some veterinarian offices and animal hospitals accept volunteers. Since these offices and hospitals aren't nonprofit groups, they tend not to have nearly as many volunteer positions as shelters, pounds, zoos, and aquariums. Also, keep in mind that if you volunteer at a veterinarian's office or hospital, you'll be helping out a business that makes money. So your time will not only help animals, it will also help a private business.

When you volunteer in these places, you'll do a variety of things, including caring for animals, cleaning their cages, and even helping prepare animals for surgery.

Inside Scoop

There are ways you can help animals other than volunteering. If you see an instance of animal cruelty, such as a dog that is chained up and rarely given food or water, report it immediately to your local humane society or other animal-help group or shelter. You might just save that animal's life. Another way you can help is by donating old blankets, towels, or pet food to an animal shelter.

Is Working with Animals for You?

As you can see, there are a great many kinds of volunteer opportunities available to you if you want to work with animals. But working with animals isn't for everyone. There are a number of pros and cons to consider.

The Pros of Volunteering to Help Animals

There are many reasons why volunteering to help animals is a great idea. Here are the most important ones:

✧ **You get to work with animals.** If you're an animal lover, you'll enjoy this kind of work. Not only will you do good, you'll have fun while doing it.

✧ **You get to immediately see the results of your volunteering.** Caring for an animal that's been abandoned, for example, is greatly satisfying—and you'll be able to see, from week to week, the progress of the animal.

❖ **You'll get back affection from the animals.** Most animals are naturally affectionate toward people, and as any pet owner knows, there's nothing like the affection of an animal. They seem to know that you're there to help them.

❖ **The hours may be flexible.** When you volunteer to help animals the hours are often flexible, making it easier to fit into your schedule.

❖ **You'll get to meet new people.** When you work with animals, you'll meet new people too. And since they're probably animal lovers as well, you'll share a common interest.

❖ **You'll find out whether you want to make it a career.** If you're thinking of becoming a veterinarian or some other profession that works with animals, there's no better way to test it out than to become a volunteer. And if you're not thinking of making it a career, you may surprise yourself and enjoy it so much that you decide to pursue it as a career.

Inside Scoop

Volunteer for a while at an animal shelter, and you'll find the animals will get to know you and look forward to your visits. When you show up, expect them to shower you with obvious shows of affection, like a whole lot of tail-wagging and face-licking from a dog or a welcoming purr from a cat.

The Cons of Volunteering to Help Animals

Volunteering to help animals isn't for everyone. It can be very demanding. Here are some cons to consider:

✧ **The work may be too physically demanding for you.** Volunteering for animals can require strength and stamina, and you may not be able to keep up.

✧ **The work can be messy.** Cleaning out cages and living areas can be a dirty and smelly job.

✧ **You could get injured.** An animal could bite or scratch you, and while it's unlikely you'll be seriously injured, it is something that you should keep in mind.

✧ **You may need to volunteer during weekends.** Perhaps you like to keep your weekends as free as possible. If so, you may not be able to do some kinds of volunteer work for animals. Zoos, for example, tend to be busiest during the weekends, so that's often when they'll want volunteers. If you'll be working directly with animals, it requires a regular commitment of time.

Information Station

Would you like to help save a rabbit? The House Rabbit Society rescues abandoned pet bunnies, cares for them, and finds them new homes. There are branches in most states in the U.S. For details, go to www.rabbit.org on the Web.

Finding a Place to Volunteer Near You

Let's say you've decided that volunteering to help animals is for you. Now it's time to find a place to volunteer. How to do it? A great place to start is with a veterinarian. If you have a pet, ask your own veterinarian for places to volunteer. He or she may even have a place for you!

If you don't have a pet, or if your pet doesn't have a regular veterinarian, check the Yellow Pages under Veterinarians. You'll find several listed. In fact, a great place to find out about volunteer opportunities for animals is in your Yellow Pages. Look under headings such as Zoos, Aquariums, Animal Shelters, Humane Societies, and similar listings. Also check the state and local government listings, which are often in the Blue Pages, a section of your local White Pages. Look for Animal Commission, Animal Control, or similar listings.

You can also call your town or city hall and explain that you want to volunteer for animals. You'll be put through to the department that can help you. Libraries are also excellent places to check.

Helping Hands

Want to help animals and the elderly at the same time? Some seniors have a difficult time caring for their animals, and might need things done such as walking a dog or caring for a cat. See if any elderly folks in your area need help caring for their pets.

Resource Guide for Volunteering for Animals

There are many places you can volunteer if you're interested in volunteering for animals. But if you're having trouble finding a place near you, don't worry—I've provided a resource guide for you to help. Here are some of the best organizations

you'll find to put you in touch with a volunteer opportunity.
I've listed the national headquarters of the organizations.
Contact the headquarters and let them know you're looking
for something in your area.

American Society for the Prevention of Cruelty to Animals (ASPCA)

The ASPCA's mission, is to "promote humane principles, prevent cruelty, and alleviate fear, pain, and suffering in animals." It's a national organization, with headquarters in New
York City, and so the only volunteer opportunities it has are
in New York. However, it's a great resource for finding shelters and humane societies in your local area. Its Web site, for
example, lists almost 5,000 local humane societies, societies
for the protection of animals, shelters, and similar places to
volunteer.

424 East 92 Street
New York, NY 10128
212-876-7700
www.aspca.org

American Veterinary Medical Association

This is an organization of veterinarians. It's a great place to
find out about animals, and to find a veterinarian near you.

1931 North Meacham Road
Schaumburg, IL 60173
847-925-8070
www.avma.org

American Zoo and Aquarium Association

This group is the main association for zoos and aquariums
across the country.

8403 Colesville Road
Suite 710
Silver Spring, MD 20910
www.aza.org

The Humane Society of the United States

This group calls itself the world's largest animal protection organization. It helps animals in many ways, from working with local shelters to educating the public about animal welfare issues.

2100 L Street NW
Washington, D.C. 20037
212-452-1100
www.hsus.org

World Wildlife Fund

This is a worldwide organization devoted to protecting wildlife and wildlands.

1250 24th Street NE
Washington, D.C. 20037
202-293-4800
www.worldwildlife.org

The Least You Need to Know

✧ You can volunteer to help animals at zoos and aquariums, town pounds and animal shelters, and animal hospitals and veterinarian offices.

✧ As a volunteer for animals, you can help feed and care for the animals, give tours, help with fund-raising, pitch in with maintenance, and help the staff.

✧ Working with animals gives you a great sense of satisfaction, as well as affection from the animals.

✧ Be aware that volunteering to help animals can be physically demanding and dirty.

Chapter 8

Volunteering for the Environment

In This Chapter

✧ What kinds of environmental dangers are there?

✧ The kinds of work you'll do as an environmental volunteer

✧ What types of environmental groups accept teen volunteers

✧ How to decide whether volunteering for the environment is for you

✧ How to find a volunteering opportunity near you

✧ Resource guide for volunteering for the environment

One of the most pressing issues facing our world today is the degradation of the environment. Dirty water and air, global warming, toxic chemicals ... the list of potential problems affecting the environment goes on and on.

You don't have to accept a degraded environment. You can do something about it. Tens of thousands of people volunteer every year to help improve the environment. As you'll see in this chapter, it's one of the most satisfying volunteering opportunities there is—and it's easy to find a place to volunteer as well.

What Kind of Work Will You Do?

If you're interested in helping save the environment, there are many different kinds of volunteer opportunities for you. You can be involved in such hands-on activities as river cleanups, research projects such as studying the activities of migrating birds, and lobbying efforts to do things such as pass stronger environmental regulations.

Before you can learn about the kinds of work you can do, though, it's a good idea to get a sense of what dangers are affecting the environment. Once you know that, it'll be easier for you to make up your mind about what kind of environmental volunteering is best for you.

Information Station

If you volunteer to help the environment, you'll probably hear the word *ecology* used a lot. Ecology refers to the relationship between living things and the environment in which they live.

What Dangers Does the Environment Face?

Entire books have been written about environmental dangers, so there's no way to adequately cover them in a few paragraphs or pages. But still, there are some basic environmental dangers that the world faces. Here are some of the primary ones:

✧ **Air pollution.** This has been a danger for many decades. While in general, the air is slowly getting cleaner, air pollution remains a major problem. Dangerous chemicals, smog, poison gases, and small airborne particles are just a few examples of air pollution. They harm our health and cause many unnecessary deaths every year.

✧ **Water pollution.** Every year chemicals, sewage, oils, heavy metals, and more stream into our rivers, lakes, and oceans. It makes water dangerous to drink or undrinkable, kills fish and other living things, and makes swimming hazardous.

✧ **Land pollution.** Roadsides are littered with trash, empty bottles and cans, and plastic. Pesticides are applied to farmers' fields in too-large amounts.

✧ **Overdevelopment.** Every year, more and more land is developed and turned into housing, stores, or used for timbering and energy development. Depleting our forests, farmlands, and waterways is a major danger, destroying animal habitat, among other problems.

✧ **Global warming.** Most scientists agree that because of all the extra carbon dioxide, methane, and other gases that we spew into the atmosphere, we're increasing the average temperature of the world. This can cause untold environmental damage, including, an increasing number of damaging hurricanes, as well as the rising of the earth's oceans because of melting glaciers and ice caps.

✧ **Dangers to biodiversity.** Biodiversity refers to the variance of plants and animals in the world. It's a fact that we're killing off plant and animal species daily. Not only does it make the earth a poorer-seeming place, it also means we won't be able to discover new medicinal drugs that are often derived from plants.

✧ **Solid waste.** As a country, we produce far too much garbage and solid waste. We're running out of landfill space. One solution—and one that draws many

volunteers—is to increase the amount of recycling that
we do. Another problem with landfills is that they
often leak into surrounding areas and waterways, often
causing pollution.

✧ **Genetically engineered foods.** Scientists have learned
how to manipulate common foods by using genetic en-
gineering. While this can be helpful—such as by creating insect-resistant vegetables that don't require the use
of pesticides—it can also carry dangers. For example,
some scientists believe that insect-resistant corn may be
killing off Monarch butterflies. And because genetically
engineered foods can carry proteins that normally
aren't found in them, people can eat food they're aller-
gic to without realizing it.

It's the Pits

You might think that a solution to our landfill problem is
to simply burn our trash in incinerators. Unfortunately,
though, incinerators contribute to major environmental
problems. They cause air pollution and can pour dangerous
heavy metals into the air.

What Kinds of Groups Help the Environment

Obviously, helping the environment is a tall order. Luckily,
there are thousands of groups across the country that work
on environmental issues, and that need volunteers. Here are
the two main kinds of groups:

1. **Governmental groups.** Federal agencies such as the
   Environmental Protection Agency (EPA) and state and

local environmental agencies tackle environmental issues. Many of them accept teen volunteers.

2. **Private groups.** Here's where most of the volunteer work comes in. You'll find an astonishing array of private groups working to help clean up the environment. These range from large well-known organizations such as the Sierra Club to small local groups that clean up neighborhoods (see Chapter 9, "Volunteering to Build Better Neighborhoods," for other volunteer opportunities in this area).

The Kinds of Work You'll Do

Now that you have a basic understanding of environmental issues and know what kinds of groups do environmental work, it's time for the nitty-gritty: learning what kinds of volunteer work you can do to help the environment. Since there are so many environmental groups and so many problems that need solving, there's no way to list most of the kinds of work you'll do. But these are among the most common:

✧ **Work on cleanups.** Many environmental groups sponsor cleanup days in which they clean parks, rivers, neighborhoods, and even collect trash along the sides of highways. These cleanups are always done by volunteers, and so volunteers are always needed.

✧ **Help with recycling programs.** One of the easiest and cheapest ways to keep the environment clean is to recycle. Most towns and cities have recycling programs and need help. When you work on a recycling program, you usually let people know that the program exists and try and get them to do more recycling.

✧ **Work with activist groups.** Countless groups work to change environmental laws and regulations and help people better understand the importance of the environment. Groups work on global warming, wilderness issues, clean air issues, saving national parks from development, saving rain forests, and many other issues that affect the environment.

Information Station

One of the oldest and best-known environmental organizations is the Sierra Club, with over 600,000 members. It helps save the environment in countless ways, and has chapters all over the country. It always needs volunteers. For more information, see "Sierra Club" in this chapter's resource guide, or send e-mail to activist.desk@sierraclub.org.

✧ **Do hands-on research and observation.** Before the environment can be protected, it has to be understood. And in order for it to be understood, it has to be studied. Many groups work to better understand how the environment works, or to try and catalog the current state of the environment. For example, in Western Massachusetts, the Audubon Society holds annual hawk counts, where volunteers count the number of hawks that migrate along the Connecticut River Valley.

✧ **Do governmental lobbying.** The laws passed by the federal, state, and local governments greatly affect the environment. Volunteers are always needed to lobby government officials, either in person or by phone or letter. Volunteers are also needed to help organize lobbying drives.

✧ **Participate in protests.** Sometimes an effective way to draw people's attention to environmental problems is to stage public protests. Volunteers are needed to participate as well as to organize protests.

✧ **Raise funds.** Private environmental groups always need help fund-raising, and for that they need volunteers. You'll help organize and participate in a variety of fund-raising events.

✧ **Do office work.** Tasks such as filing, answering the telephones, and getting things organized always needs doing in private and public environmental organizations.

✧ **Create newsletters and Web sites.** The main way that many environmental groups get the word out is by publishing information, either via newsletters or the World Wide Web. Volunteers help do both.

✧ **Do education and outreach.** The heart of what many environmental groups do is educate the public. To do that, they need volunteers to do things such as hand out pamphlets, make telephone calls, and work with the press. Some groups also need volunteers to help teach schoolchildren about the environment.

Helping Hands

Private environmental groups keep in touch with their members by sending out mailings to them, calling them by phone, and sending them newsletters. To keep track of their members, they often use databases. So if you know how to use a database, you'll be in great demand as a volunteer.

Is Environmental Volunteering for You?

As you can see, there are a great many kinds of volunteer opportunities available if you're interested in helping save the environment. But this kind of volunteer work isn't for everyone. There are a number of pros and cons to keep in mind.

Information Station

Some of the greatest wildlife and conservation parks in the world are run by the federal National Park Service. The service runs everything from the Statue of Liberty to the Point Reyes National Seashore in San Francisco, and offers many volunteer opportunities. To find them, head to www. nps.gov/volunteer on the Web.

The Pros of Volunteering for the Environment

Volunteering for the environment can be a great experience. Here are the pros of doing that kind of volunteering:

✤ **You'll be able to test out a career.** Think you're interested in going into an environmental career? There's no better way than to find out by volunteering.

✤ **You may get to work outdoors.** In many volunteering opportunities, such as doing cleanups, research, or observation, you work outside. You may even work in national and state parks. If you love the outdoors, it's a great opportunity.

✤ **You'll learn a great deal.** Volunteer to help the environment, and you'll be constantly learning about the environment and the world in which you live.

✤ **You'll get a great sense of satisfaction.** Particularly if you do something that shows immediate results, such as participating in a cleanup or recycling program, you'll get an enormous sense of satisfaction.

The Cons of Volunteering for the Environment

Volunteering for the environment isn't for everyone. Here are some cons to consider:

✧ **The work can be physically demanding.** Cleanups and clearing parks can be back-breaking work. If that kind of work isn't for you, look for environmental volunteer opportunities that are less physically demanding.

✧ **It can require many hours.** Especially if you're volunteering for a lobbying effort, it might require many hours of work, particularly if you're doing it before an election.

✧ **Activism can burn you out.** If your volunteer work involves activism or lobbying, you'll find out that burnout is always a problem. In some cases it can take years and even decades to make a difference. You may feel as if your work is of no importance, and so you can quickly tire of the work.

Finding a Place to Volunteer Near You

So let's say you've decided that volunteering for the environment is for you. Now it's time to find a place to volunteer. How to do it? As you'll see in this section, it's easy. Most environmental organizations use volunteers.

Start off with the Yellow Pages. Look under Nature Centers, Environmental Organizations, or similar listings. Also check the Blue Pages, which are the listings of local and state governments in the White Pages. You'll find many governmental environmental organizations listed. In the U.S. government listings, look for the Environmental Protection Agency. Also look for the Interior Department for listings of many environmental-related agencies, such as the National Park Service and the Fish and Wildlife Service.

Information Station

It's not only the world's environment that's endangered—many unique cultures around the world are disappearing fast. If you'd like to volunteer to help preserve world cultures, consider volunteering with Cultural Survival. Contact the Intern Program, Cultural Survival, 215 Prospect Street, Cambridge, MA 02139; 617-441-5403; www.cs.org.

Under the listings for your state government, look for the Department of Environmental Protection or a similar agency. Also check for a Fish and Wildlife department or similar agency. Under city, town, and county listings, look for parks and recreation departments, departments of environmental protection, the Department of Public Works, the conservation department, or similar listings.

Don't forget the Internet, which has many links to numerous environmental organizations. Your local library can also be a good resource.

Resource Guide for Volunteering for the Environment

There are many places you can volunteer if you're interested in working for the environment. If you're having trouble finding a place near you, don't worry—I've provided a resource guide to help you. Here are some of the best organizations—both private groups and government organizations—to help you find a volunteer opportunity. I've listed the national headquarters of the organizations. Contact the headquarters and let them know you're looking for something in your area.

Helping Hands

When trying to find the recycling program run by your city or town, start by calling the Department of Public Works. Very often, that department runs recycling programs.

Environmental Defense Fund

This group fights for the environment in many different ways, and can help you find local volunteering opportunities.

257 Park Avenue South
New York, NY 10010
212-505-2100
www.edf.org

Environmental Protection Agency

This is the federal agency charged with enforcing environmental laws. It can also put you in touch with volunteer opportunities with other groups near you.

1200 Pennsylvania Avenue NW
Washington, D.C. 20460
www.epa.gov

Keep America Beautiful

This group works to fight litter and promote recycling.

1010 Washington Boulevard
Stamford, CT 06901
203-323-8987
www.kab.org

It's the Pits

Before volunteering at an environmental group, research it carefully, especially how it gets its funds. Sometimes groups that say they're out to help the environment may in fact *fight* against environmental regulations. Sometimes polluters form groups that sound environmentally friendly, but in fact aren't.

Kids for a Clean Environment (Kids F.A.C.E.)

This environmental kids' organization is a great place to turn to find out how you can volunteer to help the environment.

P.O. Box 158254
Nashville, TN 37215
615-331-7381
www.kidsface.org

National Park Service

This federal agency runs the U.S. National Parks. There are many national parks, and not just in wilderness areas. Many cities such as New York and Boston have areas run by the National Park Service

1849 C Street NW
Washington, D.C. 20240
202-208-6843
www.nps.gov

National Wildlife Federation

This is one of the largest and most effective environmental organizations. It uses volunteers, and can also help you find other volunteer opportunities near you.

8925 Leesburg Pike
Vienna, VA 22184
703-790-4000
www.nwf.org

Sierra Club

The Sierra Club is one of the oldest and best-known environmental organizations. It has volunteer opportunities of its own, and can also guide you to other opportunities.

Sierra Club
Office of Volunteer and Activist Services
85 Second Street
San Francisco, CA 94105
www.sierraclub.com

The Student Conservation Association

This private group offers exceptional volunteer opportunities for teens. You'll do things such as build a cabin in Vermont's Merck Forest and Farmland Center, or restore vegetation at campsites in Yosemite National Park.

P.O. Box 550
Charlestown, NH 03603
603-543-1700
www.sca-inc.org

The Least You Need to Know

✧ The two primary types of groups that work on helping the environment are government groups such as the Environmental Protection Agency, and private groups such as the Sierra Club.

✧ Among the kinds of work you'll do are cleanups, outreach and education, working as an activist, and doing field research and observation.

✧ Volunteering for the environment is great if you like working outdoors.

✧ This type of volunteering can be physically demanding, so if you're not physically fit, make sure the volunteering opportunity is right for you.

✧ Check the Blue Pages of the phone book to find governmental environmental organizations near you, as well as the Internet and your local library.

Chapter 9

Volunteering to Build Better Neighborhoods

In This Chapter

✧ The different types of groups that help improve neighborhoods

✧ What you'll do when you volunteer to build better neighborhoods

✧ Deciding whether volunteering to help neighborhoods is for you

✧ How you can find a way to volunteer to improve neighborhoods

✧ Resource guide for volunteering to build better neighborhoods

There's a popular bumper sticker you might have seen that says "Think Globally, Act Locally." There's a lot of truth in that statement. Often, the best way to save the world is to start with the places closest to you. What is a town, a city, or even a country, after all, but a collection of many neighborhoods? So when you volunteer to build better neighborhoods, you're really volunteering to help build a better world.

You don't have to volunteer only in your neighborhood. Very often, your volunteer work will take you to other neighborhoods that might need your help more. In this chapter, you'll find everything you need to know about volunteering to build better neighborhoods.

The Types of Groups That Build Better Neighborhoods

There are many different ways to volunteer to build better neighborhoods. Very often, the neighborhoods you'll help are poor and neglected. Houses need to be refurbished and updated, streets cleaned, and the neighborhood's safety maintained.

Before you can find out what kind of work you can do, let's learn a bit about the groups that work to improve neighborhoods. There are three general categories:

1. **Government organizations.** From local to state to county to federal government, many organizations help neighborhoods. They spend money on updating housing, pass and enforce laws about building safety, and participate in renewal projects in which money is spent on helping particular neighborhoods. The main federal agency that helps build better neighborhoods is the department of Housing and Urban Development, often referred to as HUD.

2. **Nonprofit groups.** Many private, nonprofit groups help build better neighborhoods in many different ways. Habitat for Humanity International, for example, builds houses for people who otherwise couldn't afford them. Keep America Beautiful works to clean up and beautify neighborhoods. There are many other examples as well. These national groups have local chapters in your area.

3. **Local groups.** Countless local groups, such as a Kiwanis Club or Rotary Club, work on building better neighborhoods. Churches and synagogues do a great deal of

work in building better neighborhoods. Many other organizations also do this kind of work, such as grass-roots neighborhood groups. For example, for years I've been a volunteer for the Porter Square Neighbor's Association, a group in my neighborhood that works on neighborhood issues such as making traffic patterns safer and making sure that the redevelopment of a shopping center is good for the neighborhood.

Inside Scoop

Neighborhood groups often work with local businesses to build better neighborhoods, to the benefit of both. For example, Cambridge's Porter Square Neighbor's Association worked closely with a shopping center to make sure it was redeveloped in a way the neighborhood wanted. The result also benefited the shopping center, since people were happier to shop there.

What You'll Do as a Volunteer

Now that you have a basic understanding of the groups that help build better neighborhoods, it's time to see what kinds of volunteer work you can do. Since there are so many neighborhood groups and so many problems that need solving, there's no way to list all of the kinds of work you'll do, but these are among the most common:

✧ **Work on neighborhood cleanups.** This is one of the most popular kinds of volunteer jobs for helping neighborhoods. You go into a neighborhood and pick up the trash; plant trees, flowers, and other plants; get rid of

111

weeds; water plants; paint murals; and more. Some organizations also have "Adopt-a-Highway" or "Adopt-a-Spot" programs in which they clean and beautify a stretch of highway or an area in a neighborhood.

✧ **Build housing.** One of the most successful neighborhood betterment organizations is Habitat for Humanity International. This group uses volunteers to build housing for people who otherwise couldn't afford it. Since its founding in 1976, it's built over 100,000 houses in over 60 countries. More than 30,000 of those houses were built in the United States. Even if you're all thumbs and don't have a clue about how to build a house, you can volunteer for this organization or others like it.

✧ **Raise funds.** It's tough to improve neighborhoods without money. And so most neighborhood-betterment groups need fund-raising help—and lots of it. You'll participate and help plan fund-raising events. You may also ask businesses to donate supplies such as rakes, shovels, and plants that can help beautify neighborhoods.

✧ **Help small neighborhood groups.** Many small neighborhood groups need help with everything from knocking on doors to educate people about neighborhood issues to making calls about upcoming meetings.

✧ **Do office work.** Neighborhood groups need people willing to help around the office, doing such tasks as answering telephones, filing, working with computers, and sending out mailings.

✧ **Educate the public.** Neighborhood groups depend heavily on the public for help in everything from neighborhood cleanups to attending public meetings that affect neighborhoods. To spur people to action, they need volunteers to make phone calls, hand out pamphlets, and knock on people's doors to educate people and raise funds.

✧ **Work on newsletters and the Web.** One of the best ways neighborhood groups have of letting the world know what they're doing—and of getting help—is to create and distribute newsletters, and publish sites on the World Wide Web. They need your help to write and produce the newsletter and build pages on the Web.

✧ **Be an activist.** Sometimes, in order to help a neighborhood, people are needed to draw attention to specific problems. Activists might attend and speak at public meetings or attend protests or other public-information events.

Helping Hands

Some neighborhoods fight crime by having Neighborhood Watch programs, in which private citizens patrol the streets at night and report any problems to the police. These programs always need help. Contact your local police to see if there's one near you.

Is Volunteering to Help Neighborhoods for You?

As you can see, there are a great many volunteer opportunities available if you want to help build better neighborhoods. But volunteering for neighborhoods isn't for everyone. There are a number of pros and cons to consider.

Helping Hands

In order for neighborhood groups to succeed they need lots of volunteers. One thing volunteers often do is recruit more volunteers by letting friends and people at school know about the group.

The Pros of Volunteering to Build Better Neighborhoods

Volunteering to help build better neighborhoods can be a great experience. Here are the pros of doing that kind of work:

✦ **You'll be able to test out a career.** Think you're interested in helping neighborhoods as a career? There's no better way than to find out by volunteering.

✦ **You may get to work outdoors.** In many volunteering opportunities to help neighborhoods, such as doing cleanups, you work outside. If you love working outside, it's a great opportunity.

✦ **You can learn construction skills.** Barely know how to use a hammer, but you'd like to learn construction skills? There's no better way to learn than by doing. If you volunteer to help build or repair homes, you'll become well-versed in home construction and repair.

✦ **You'll get the satisfaction of seeing the immediate results of your work.** Build a house where there was none, and you'll see in vivid detail how volunteering can pay off. Better still, you'll know you've built a house for someone who otherwise would not be able to afford it. There are few greater satisfactions in life than helping others.

✧ **The work you'll do is fun.** Cleaning up neighborhoods, building houses … when you do this kind of work, not only will you be doing good, but you'll have fun as well. You'll work with a large group of people who enjoy being together and you'll make new friends.

✧ **You'll make friends in your neighborhood.** Life is so busy that it can be hard to know your neighbors. When you work to better your neighborhood, you'll meet them and make new friends who live near you.

It's the Pits

If you're going to be working on neighborhood cleanups or construction and repair, keep in mind that the work is often dirty. Don't wear good clothes—old jeans and sweatshirts are best.

The Cons of Volunteering to Build Better Neighborhoods

Volunteering to build better neighborhoods isn't for everyone. Here are some of the cons:

✧ **The work can be physically demanding.** Cleanups, construction, and repair can be back-breaking work. If that kind of work isn't for you, look for neighborhood-bettering opportunities that don't require heavy physical labor.

✧ **It can require many hours.** Building a house in particular can require a serious time commitment. You may
not be willing or able to devote that much time.

✧ **You may not like working closely with others.** Most
of the things that you'll do when you build better
neighborhoods will require group effort. If you're the
kind of person who would rather work alone, consider
other kinds of volunteering opportunities.

Finding a Place to Volunteer Near You

Let's say you've decided that volunteering to build better
neighborhoods is for you. Now it's time to find a place to
volunteer. A great place to start is with a church or syna-
gogue. Many have programs for helping neighborhoods. Or
try the Yellow Pages and look for listings such as Community
Groups and Service Organizations. Check the Blue Pages,
which are the listings of local, state, and federal governments
in the White Pages. In the U.S. government listings, look for
the department of Housing and Urban Development (HUD).
In city listings, look for the Department of Public Works, a
local housing authority, and community center listings.

Helping Hands

A great way to find out how you can help in your neighborhood is to call the mayor's office, or your town or city
councilors. They'll have a list of organizations that could
use your help.

Also ask your parents what organizations they belong to, and
find out if any of them sponsor neighborhood-betterment

work. Check with your guidance counselor as well—they usually have lists of neighborhood organizations that need volunteers.

One of the best places to turn is your local library. Ask the reference librarian for a list of neighborhood organizations near you. Newspapers are a big help as well. Neighborhood organizations frequently publicize their activities in newspapers. The more local the newspaper, the more likely it is to cover these kinds of groups. Some local weekly newspapers also devote different sections to specific neighborhoods, so look in those neighborhood sections first. Check in with service organizations such as Kiwanis Clubs, Rotary Clubs, and similar groups, too. They almost always sponsor neighborhood-betterment programs.

Inside Scoop

I can tell you from personal experience that if you want to find volunteer opportunities, local weekly newspapers are the best place to turn. I used to be editor-in-chief of a chain of local weekly newspapers in the Boston area, and I always made sure that my reporters regularly covered anything that neighborhood groups did.

Resource Guide for Volunteering for Better Neighborhoods

There are many places you can volunteer if you're interested in volunteering to build better neighborhoods. If you're having trouble finding a place near you, don't worry—I've provided a resource guide to help you. Here are some of the best organizations—both private groups and government organizations—to help you find a volunteer opportunity. I've listed the national headquarters of the organizations. Contact the headquarters and let them know you're looking for something in your area.

AmeriCares

Among this group's many programs is AmeriCares Homefront, a program that helps repair homes across the country for those who need help.

161 Cherry Street
New Canaan, CT 06840
1-800-486-4357
www.americares.org

Christmas in April

This organization preserves and revitalizes housing and neighborhoods across the country for those who need help.

1536 16th Street NW
Washington, D.C. 20036
202-483-9081
www.christmasinapril.org

Habitat for Humanity International

This extraordinary group builds or rehabilitates housing for the needy across the country. The recipients of the house work alongside volunteers to help build or rehabilitate their homes.

121 Habitat Street
Americus, GA 31709
1-800-HABITAT
www.habitat.org

Keep America Beautiful

This group works to fight litter and to beautify America.

1010 Washington Boulevard
Stamford, CT 06901
203-323-8987
www.kab.org

Information Station

Keeping your neighborhood clean can start at home and in your school—and there are things you can do on your own, without having to join a larger organization. Go to www.kab.org/kids1.cfm for some tips from the Keep America Beautiful group on what you can do.

Kids for a Clean Environment (Kids F.A.C.E.)

This environmental kids' organization is a great place to turn to find out how you can volunteer to clean up neighborhoods.

P.O. Box 158254
Nashville, TN 37215
615-331-7381
www.kidsface.org

U.S. Department of Housing and Urban Development (HUD)

This is the main federal agency that helps build better neighborhoods. It's a great resource for finding volunteer opportunities not only with HUD, but with other groups as well. For a comprehensive listing of volunteer opportunities for HUD and other places, head to www.hud.gov/volunter.html.

451 7th Street SW
Washington, D.C. 20410
202-708-1112
www.hud.gov

The Least You Need to Know

✧ Three types of groups help build better neighborhoods: government agencies, nonprofit groups, and small, local organizations.

✧ Among the things you'll do if you want to build better neighborhoods is participate in cleanups and build and repair homes for the needy.

✧ When you volunteer to build or repair homes, you'll learn a variety of construction skills, even if you can barely hold a hammer now.

✧ Volunteering to help neighborhoods can be messy and physically demanding, but it's satisfying to see the immediate impact you can make on upgrading a neighborhood.

✧ An excellent place to volunteer is with Habitat for Humanity International, which builds and repairs houses for the needy. You can find them on the Web at www. habitat.org.

Chapter 10

Volunteering for the Arts and in Museums

In This Chapter

✧ What kinds of volunteer work you can do in art museums, science museums, and history museums

✧ What kinds of volunteer work you can do for performing arts organizations

✧ How to decide whether volunteering for the arts and in museums is for you

✧ Finding a volunteer experience for the arts and in museums near you

✧ Resource guide for volunteers for the arts and in museums

In just about every city and town across the country there are arts museums, other kinds of museums such as science and history museums, theater companies, opera companies, and many other kinds of arts organizations.

Most of them need your help. If you have an interest in the arts or museums, you'll find many different kinds of volunteering opportunities awaiting you. Read on for the inside scoop on what to do, where to go, and how to do it.

What Kinds of Work Will You Do?

Whether you have artistic flair or can't draw a straight line, study the piano or can't play a note, go to museums regularly or rarely attend—you'll find an almost mind-boggling variety of ways to volunteer for the arts and in museums. You can help raise funds, educate the public, work in a gift shop, serve as a tour guide, help construct scenery, and much more.

In general, there are three kinds of places where you can volunteer, described in the following sections.

Arts Museums and Other Organizations

If you are interested in the arts, there are many volunteer opportunities for you at art museums and other organizations devoted to art. When you volunteer at these places, not only will you help others, you'll also help yourself, whether or not you plan a career in the arts. You will better understand the arts, and that will allow you to lead a fuller life, with an enjoyment of a wide variety of experiences.

Inside Scoop

If you plan to volunteer at a museum of any sort, you may hear the term "docent." That's just a fancy term for someone who gives guided tours at a museum.

When you volunteer in an arts museum, you'll learn a lot about art. If you're going to be a tour guide, you'll be taught about the exhibits and trained in how to be a guide. If you'll be working behind the scenes, you'll learn about the inner workings of a museum.

Information Station

Museums and nonprofit groups aren't the only places to turn for volunteering. Check with local arts galleries. Even though galleries are for-profit companies, they sometimes need volunteers.

If you're interested in volunteering in the visual arts, there are more opportunities than museums. Many cities and towns have arts councils, and these councils need all different kinds of volunteers to do things such as get publicity, organize arts fairs, or set up exhibits. State governments often have arts councils as well.

While there are many different kinds of volunteering you can do, here are the most common ways you can volunteer at art museums and other art institutions:

✧ **Be a tour guide.** Museums always need people to guide visitors through exhibits and the museum itself. You may become a guide for a specific exhibit, or a more general guide to help people get around within the museum.

✧ **Help raise funds.** The arts never have enough funding in the United States, and so museums and other arts groups frequently have fund-raisers. You can help out with fund-raising by organizing events, helping with mailings, and similar kinds of work.

✧ **Help paint murals.** In many cities and towns, arts organizations have painted murals that beautify neighborhoods and extend the arts into people's lives. Volunteers often help paint those murals. Painting a mural is a great experience—it's fun, productive, satisfying, and a great way to meet and work with people.

✧ **Work in the museum gift shop.** Museums generally have gift shops that sell posters, artwork, books, and other goods. They frequently need people to volunteer to work in the shops as sales clerks.

✧ **Help the museum staff.** There's always filing that needs to be done, phone calls that need to be made, artwork to be cataloged, and similar jobs.

✧ **Help with outreach.** Many art museums and arts organizations recognize that they can't rely solely on people to go to museums—they also have to bring museums to the people. So there are many different kinds of community outreach. People bring artwork and talk about artwork in schools, senior centers, and other places. Neighborhood and city-wide arts festivals are held, and they rely heavily on volunteers.

✧ **Work on short-term projects.** Special exhibitions, programs, events, and similar activities are always cropping up. Volunteers are always needed.

✧ **Help with conservation and curating.** Works of art are precious things that can easily be damaged. They need to be preserved and cared for, and sometimes volunteers can help with these tasks. Volunteers can also help curators in planning and setting up exhibits.

✧ **Work on getting publicity.** Arts museums and organizations need publicity to let people know about their exhibits and activities. You can help by writing press releases, creating a Web site, making phone calls, and similar activities.

✧ **Work with museum members.** Museums offer memberships to people, who receive benefits such as newsletters and invitations to special events. You can help write and publish newsletters, and assist in other membership activities such as membership drives.

Inside Scoop

A big arts festival, the River Festival, is held every year on the banks of the Charles River in Massachusetts. Hundreds of volunteers, including many teens, do everything from making giant puppets for the parade to helping publicize the festival. Look for a similar festival in your area and volunteer your talents!

Performing Arts Organizations

No matter what your talents or experience, there are many opportunities for you in performing arts organizations such as symphonies, operas, theaters, and dance companies. By volunteering, I'm not talking about actually performing. No matter how talented you may be, that's not really a community service. What I'm talking about here is helping performing arts organizations do their job better.

While there are many different ways you can help, here are some of the most common:

✧ **Work as an usher.** Help is needed handing out programs as people walk in and showing people to their seats.

✧ **Sew costumes and work on scenery**. A lot that you don't see goes into any theater, dance, or opera production. Help is always needed sewing costumes and building or painting scenery.

✧ **Help with fund-raising.** Any performing arts organization you can name requires outside help. That means fund-raising. These groups always need volunteers to work on fund drives, make phone calls, and other associated fund-raising activities.

It's the Pits

It may be more difficult to do cool things like sew costumes and build scenery in larger, professional performing arts groups, because these groups have professionals work on costumes and scenery. Smaller groups often turn to volunteers for help

✧ **Help with outreach.** Performing arts groups often perform in the community, particularly in schools. They need volunteers to help with that and other kinds of community outreach.

✧ **Work in the gift shop.** Dance companies and opera companies, as well as other performing arts groups, usually have a gift shop. They need people to help out.

✧ **Help with public relations.** If people don't come to a performance, there is no show. And the best way to get people to come is by publicizing the event. Groups need help with public relations by helping put together and mail press releases.

✧ **Work with subscribers.** Many performing arts groups rely heavily on subscribers—people who pay for an entire season of performances. Subscribers get more than just tickets to the shows—they often get extra perks, such as entry to members-only events and newsletters. Groups need help in hosting the events and producing the newsletters.

Helping Hands

If you're interested in a career in the performing arts—or if you just want to perform for fun—volunteering is a great way to make contacts. Who knows, if you hang around enough, you just might end up on stage!

Science, History, and Other Museums

Many kinds of museums—not just art museums—need your volunteer help, including history museums, natural history museums, science museums, and historic houses. You'll do similar kinds of work in each, such as guiding tours or helping to raise funds. However, there are some other things you can do as well:

✧ **Help children and schools with hands-on exhibits.** Science museums in particular feature many hands-on exhibits where children can interact with the exhibits. Museums need volunteers to help children and schools with these kinds of exhibits.

✧ **Work as a research assistant.** Many science, natural history, and history museums do a great deal of research and need volunteers to serve as research assistants. Research assistants may help write lab reports, file paperwork, help in biology labs, and more.

✧ **Help out on "science nights."** Many museums have special events like "science nights" or astronomy nights for children and families. Some even offer occasional sleepovers right in the museum. Volunteers are always needed for these events.

Inside Scoop

"Living history" sites are places where an entire historical village may be reconstructed, with people dressed in the clothing of an earlier time. They even speak in the language. A popular one is Plymouth Plantation in Massachusetts, which recreates a Puritan village. Some of these museums accept volunteer help—check one out for a fun volunteering experience.

Is Volunteering for the Arts and in Museums for You?

As you can see, there are a great many kinds of volunteer opportunities available to you if you want to volunteer for the arts and in museums. But this kind of volunteering isn't everyone's cup of tea. There are a number of pros and cons to keep in mind.

The Pros of Volunteering for the Arts and in Museums

Volunteering for the arts and in museums can be a great experience. Here are all the pros of doing that kind of volunteering:

✧ **It'll give you an inside track to the arts.** Ask anyone involved with the arts professionally, and he or she will tell you it's almost impossible to break in. Volunteering is a great way to get your foot in the door. You'll develop contacts, get real-world experience, understand how the arts business works—and volunteering looks great on a resumé.

✧ **You'll work with interesting people.** Museums and arts-related organizations are full of vital, interesting people who you might not otherwise meet.

✧ **It'll give you insight into a science or history career.** Volunteering at a science or history museum is a great way to break into the science or history field.

✧ **You'll develop confidence in public speaking.** The greatest fear many people have is speaking in public. If you become a museum volunteer, you'll be trained to give tours. It's a good way to overcome a fear of public speaking. And being able to speak to a group of people is a good skill to have later in life.

✧ **You may get free classes or free tickets to shows.** Some museums and arts centers also give many kinds of classes. If you volunteer at the museum or arts center, you may be able to attend the classes without having to pay tuition. And sometimes, all you have to do is work in a gift shop or snack shop during intermission to get a free ticket to the show.

The Cons of Volunteering for the Arts and in Museums

Volunteering for the arts in museums isn't for everyone. Here are some of the cons to consider:

✧ **You may feel uncomfortable around performers and artists.** Performers and artists can be flamboyant and eccentric people. (I'm married to a painter, so I speak from experience.) If you're uncomfortable around those kind of people, this kind of volunteering isn't for you.

✧ **It can take up your weekends.** Many performances take place on the weekends. That means you'll have to volunteer on the weekends, which can take up a good portion of your free time.

✧ **You may be shy and not want to be a guide.** If you're uncomfortable speaking in public—and don't want to overcome that shyness—then you won't want to be a museum guide.

Finding a Place to Volunteer Near You

Let's say you've decided that volunteering for the arts and in museums is for you. Now it's time to find a place to volunteer. Start close to home, with your parents. Do they go to museums, the theater, concerts, or other performing arts? If so, ask them where. Then make a call and say you're interested in volunteering.

Next stop: the trusty Yellow Pages. Look under Museums, Theater, Dance, Opera, Orchestras, and Symphonies. Check the Blue Pages also, which are the listings of local and state governments in the White Pages. See if there's an arts council or similar organization in your town. If you live in a city that has state government offices, look for whatever department handles the arts.

Don't forget the Internet, which has many links to the arts and museums. Another good place to turn is your local library.

Information Station

A great way to find a list of museums near you is on the Web, on the Virtual Library's Museums in the USA page (www.museumca.org/usa). There, you'll find a state-by-state listing of museums across the country.

Resource Guide for Volunteering for the Arts

There are many places you can volunteer if you're interested in volunteering for the arts and in museums. The following resource guide will help you track down an opportunity. I've listed the national headquarters of the organizations. Contact the headquarters and let them know you're looking for something in your area.

National Endowment for the Arts

The National Endowment for the Arts is a federal agency that supports the arts in the United States, giving out grants to many local arts agencies and artists.

1100 Pennsylvania Avenue NW
Washington, D.C. 20506
202-682-5400
www.nea.gov

National Endowment for the Humanities

The National Endowment for the Humanities is a federal agency that supports the humanities in the United States, giving out grants to many museums and arts agencies.

1100 Pennsylvania Avenue NW
Washington, D.C. 20506
202-606-8400
www.neh.gov

Western States Arts Federation (WESTAF)

WESTAF is a nonprofit organization dedicated to promoting and preserving the arts in Alaska, Arizona, California, Colorado, Idaho, Montana, Nevada, New Mexico, Oregon, Utah, Washington, and Wyoming.

1543 Champa Street
Suite 220
Denver, CO 80202
303-629-1166
www.westaf.org

The Least You Need to Know

✧ Many museums need volunteers to help give tours, so when you volunteer in one, you'll learn a great deal about the arts, science, or history.

✧ Museums often need volunteers to help with outreach to schools, senior centers, and other parts of the community.

✧ Smaller performing arts groups often need volunteers to help sew costumes or build scenery, but larger professional groups in big cities may not need that kind of help.

✧ To find a place to volunteer, check with your local town arts council, look on the Internet, or check your public library.

Chapter 11

Volunteering in Politics and Government

In This Chapter

✧ The different ways you can make a difference by volunteering in government and politics

✧ How to decide whether to volunteer in government and politics

✧ Finding volunteer opportunities in government and politics near you

✧ Resource guide for volunteering in government and politics

If you're interested in helping others, changing the world, and feeling that you're directing life instead of having it direct you, then you should consider volunteering in government and politics. Government and politics affect every aspect of our lives, from driving on the highways to getting our mail delivered to paying taxes. Government plays a major role in helping the needy as well.

One great thing about this kind of volunteer work is that it lets you make a difference in people's lives, both short and long term. That's because the work you do will help shape the direction in which the country moves.

As you'll see in this chapter, if you're interested in volunteering in government or politics, there's a lot you can do.

What Kinds of Work Will You Do?

Politics generally means an attempt to win public office in a level or government or to influence the way government does things. There are two different ways people can be involved in politics:

1. **Through running for public office.** From the president down through Congress, state government offices, mayors, and even in some towns, the dog catcher, public offices are elected. People run for public office by making promises that they'll do things better.

2. **Through public interest or advocacy groups.** Running for public office is only one way to affect how government is managed. Many people, in fact, believe that there's a lot more effective ways to change things about the government than by running for public office. One way is to work with a public interest or advocacy group. There are literally thousands of these groups, such as groups that pressure the government to pay more attention to the environment or to lower taxes.

Volunteering in Government

Now that you know what government does and what politics is, where do you fit in? How can you help? If you want to volunteer in government, there are countless opportunities open to you. Here are the kinds of things you'll be able to do:

✧ **Work for your mayor.** Mayors are often deluged by requests from people who need help in many different ways. They have a hard time cataloging and answering all the requests, such as getting help if someone's heat has been cut off. Volunteers can help by gathering the requests for the mayor's office.

Helping Hands

In cities, mayors are usually the chief executive officers and are elected. But in many towns, there's a Town Manager or something similar. The Town Manager usually isn't elected, but appointed by the town council. Town Managers need volunteers too, so if you live in a town without a mayor, see if you can volunteer for the Town Manager.

➢ **Work for the city or town council.** City and town councils make local laws, rules, and regulations. They are often elected from specific neighborhoods, and this means that city and town councilors get many requests from their neighborhood—about such things as making sure snowy streets are plowed, for example. They need people to field the calls and help solve people's problems.

➢ **Answer phone calls and do other office work.** Government offices of all types field phone calls all day long. Usually, the phone call is for a simple thing such as finding the name and address of an agency that can help with a problem. Volunteers can help field those phone calls and answer questions.

➢ **Sort the mail.** Nope, this isn't a glamorous job, but someone's got to do it. Often, the way to get a start in volunteering for government is to do this mundane but very important task.

✧ **Answer the mail.** Elected officials frequently get mail asking that they vote a certain way—or congratulating or berating them. Officials would like every one of those pieces of mail answered. The answer is usually a form letter. Someone has to read each letter and decide which form letter to send—and to decide when a letter requires a more personal answer.

✧ **Help with special events.** Governments are always setting up special events, such as public celebrations or drives to feed the hungry. They need volunteers to do much of the work for organizing these events.

✧ **Do research for legislators.** Legislators—ranging from city councilors to state legislators and all the way up to Congress—always need research done. They need to research issues so that they can decide how to vote on issues and how to draft legislation.

✧ **Attend meetings.** Government seems to thrive on meetings. Legislative meetings, executive meetings … meetings, meetings, and more meetings! Someone needs to attend them and take notes on what occurs.

✧ **Build Web sites.** When it comes to technology and the Internet, government is often behind the times. Legislators, mayors, and government offices all need help communicating with people, and one of the best ways to do that is to build a Web site.

✧ **Help local, state, and federal agencies.** Elected offices get all the publicity, but it's government agencies that do all the work, such as protecting the environment and helping the needy. Many of them rely on volunteers to help get the work done.

✧ **Do everything under the sun.** The truth is, if you volunteer for government, you may end up doing just about anything. The work changes from day to day, especially if you work for a legislator. You could be a chauffeur one day, a researcher the next, and a project manager the next. One thing's for sure: You'll never be bored!

Information Station

One of the more interesting government volunteer opportunities you'll find is with the U.S. Department of Housing and Urban Development's Neighborhood Networks. The program runs centers in low-income housing projects and areas to teach people how to use computers. It needs many volunteers. Contact Neighborhood Networks, 9300 Lee Highway, Fairfax, VA 22031; 1-888-312-2743; www. neighborhoodnetworks.org.

Volunteering in Politics

Here's a secret you might not know: Political campaigns, at least on the local level, rely on volunteers more than they do on money. They need volunteers to make phone calls, to turn out the vote, to write and distribute flyers, to raise money, to get publicity … in short, to do everything of importance.

And it's not just people running for public office who need volunteers. Public interest groups and advocacy groups need volunteers just as badly. In short, the politics of this country is run by people like you—people who care and who want to contribute their time.

Information Station

For more information about politics, political campaigns, interest groups, and ways to volunteer, head to www.voter. com and click on Activism.

There are many different things that volunteers can do in political campaigns and for interest groups and advocacy groups. Here are some of the most common:

✧ **Get out the vote.** Voting is what political campaigns are all about, and it's what makes this country run. Volunteers are always needed to help encourage people to vote. There are many different organizations that help get out the vote, from people running for office to non-profit groups such as the League of Women Voters and the National Association for the Advancement of Colored People (NAACP).

✧ **Do fund-raising.** Any political campaign needs money. Volunteers help with fund-raising efforts, doing everything from making phone calls to organizing fund-raisers.

✧ **Educate the public.** Interest groups and advocacy groups spend a great deal of time educating the public about the issues. They need people to write literature, hand out pamphlets, make phone calls, and talk to the press, among other tasks.

✧ **Work on newsletters and create Web sites.** Politicians and interest groups need to stay in touch with voters, and they do it through newsletters and Web sites. They need people to write and publish the newsletters and create the Web sites.

✧ **Send out mailings.** A common way to spur people to action is by sending out mailings. Someone needs to stuff the envelopes and send them out—and that usually means volunteers.

✧ **Answer telephones and do office work.** Telephone calls need to be made all the time—everything from requests for help to fund-raising. And there is always filing and other general office work to be done. In particular, computer skills are welcomed. If you have them, especially working with databases, the campaigns want you.

Is Volunteering in Politics and Government for You?

As you can see, there are many kinds of volunteer opportunities available if you want to volunteer in the government and politics. But volunteering in this area isn't for everyone. There are a number of pros and cons to keep in mind.

The Pros of Volunteering in Government and Politics

Volunteering in government and in politics can be a great experience. Here are all the pros of doing that kind of work:

✧ **You'll know that you've made a difference.** Government and politics touch the lives of virtually everyone in the United States, so one of the best ways to make a difference in the world is to help out in this area.

✧ **You'll be able to find out if politics and government are for you.** Think you might want to go into politics or government? There's no better way than to volunteer now for the real inside scoop on how it all works.

✧ **You'll make great contacts.** People in politics and government are often great networkers—they tend to know a wide variety of people. Even if you don't plan to go into politics and government, they can probably help you in the future.

✧ **You won't feel as cynical about the world.** Everyone complains about politics and the government, but very few people actually do anything about it. When you've actually tried to change things, you'll feel less cynical about the world.

✧ **You'll get to know a wide variety of people.** More than just about any other work you can do, volunteering in politics and government exposes you to the widest number and variety of people possible.

Information Station

Many cities and towns have Youth Commissions government organizations devoted to issues facing youth. These commissions are usually made up of teens, at least in part. If you're interested in politics and government, call your local town or city hall and ask how to become part of the commission.

The Cons of Volunteering in Government and Politics

Volunteering in government and politics isn't for everyone. Here are some cons to think about:

✧ **You can be put under extreme pressure.** Political campaigns are pressure cookers, in which a single misstep could spell the difference between victory and defeat. Even volunteer opportunities tend to put you in very high-pressure situations.

✦ **You may have to work long hours.** When you work on a political campaign, you may be called on to work long hours, especially toward the end of the campaign. If your schedule doesn't allow you to work long hours, or if you simply don't want to work long hours, volunteering in a political campaign might not be for you.

✦ **You can find yourself in the middle of political controversies.** By volunteering at a government agency, you could find yourself in the middle of a political controversy simply because you happen to work there. When you answer the phones, for example, you may find yourself the subject of ire.

✦ **You don't like working closely with people.** Most of the volunteer opportunities in government and politics require that you work closely with others as part of a team. If this doesn't suit your personality, this kind of volunteering isn't for you.

Finding a Place to Volunteer Near You

So you've decided that volunteering in government and politics is for you. Now what? If you're interested in electoral politics, read your local newspapers and research who's about to run for public office. Find out where they stand on the issues. Decide which candidate fits with your own point of view on the issues, then check with Directory Assistance to contact that person. You'll also probably find posters, flyers, and other volunteers around, so you can find out information that way as well.

Also check the newspapers for the names of local public interest and advocacy groups. It shouldn't take you long to find them—if the group is a well-run one, it will get quoted all the time. When you find names, call up Directory Assistance to ask for the phone number. You can also call your local Democratic, Republican, or other party. It will be more than willing to tell you the names of candidates and to accept you as a volunteer.

Call your town or city hall and ask for the mayor's office and town councilor or city council offices. Then call the office and say you want to volunteer. Also check the Blue Pages of your phone book, which has a listing of all the government offices in your area, from local to county, city, state, and federal. It's the best single place for a comprehensive list of places you can call to volunteer.

Helping Hands

Here's a great way to get involved with politics and government: Start at your own school. Even if you don't run for office in your student government, there's still a lot of work you can do, such as getting involved with your student council.

Ask your parents and their friends if they have any connections. A surprising number of people have connections to elected officials and government offices. The reference desk of your local library will be a big help as well. You might want to start with your local League of Women Voters, an organization that educates people about public policy and encourages them to vote (see the following resource guide for contact information).

Resource Guide for Volunteering in Government and Politics

There are many thousands of government offices, political candidates, public interest groups, and advocacy groups. The ones listed here are some of the more well-known ones and only a start. Use this guide to help find places to volunteer near you.

Democratic National Committee

This is the official organization of the Democratic party. It will help you find local Democratic candidates near you if you want to volunteer for them.

430 S. Capitol Street SE
Washington, D.C. 20003
202-863-8000
www.democrats.org

League of Women Voters

This well-known organization educates people about public policy and encourages them to vote. It has chapters in many states and cities.

1730 M S
Suite 100(
Washingt(
202-429-1
www.lwv.c

Project Vote

This superb
the best res
you find ou
representati

www.vote-sr

144

www.whitehouse.gov

agency. Click on Gateway

has a comprehensive lis

more than just findi

The White House

White House O

www.vote

click

for

It's the Pits

It's easy to get carried away when volunteering in politics, especially if you volunteer for an advocacy group. But make sure that you don't get pressured to do anything you don't believe in, such as breaking the law to get across your point.

Republican National Committee

This is the official organization of the Republican party. It will help you find local Republican candidates near you if you want to volunteer for them.

310 First Street SE
Washington, D.C. 20003
202-863-8500
www.rnc.org

Voter.com

Here's another Web site that's a great resource for everything to do with politics and government. It's particularly helpful finding public interest groups and advocacy groups. Just on Activism for a list.

r.com

nline

as an official Web site that's great for g out about the White House. It also ing to just about every federal o Government for all the details.

The Least You Need to Know

✧ You can volunteer at the local, state, or federal level of government.

✧ If you're interested in volunteering in politics, you'll either volunteer for candidates or for public interest or advocacy groups.

✧ Many volunteers for elected officials answer telephones and respond to citizen's requests and comments.

✧ When you volunteer for elected officials, you'll get to work with a wide variety of people from every walk of life.

✧ Political campaigns are exciting places to volunteer, but the work tends to be high-pressure and can require long hours.

✧ Read your local newspaper to find out about local candidates, public interest groups, and advocacy groups that are looking for volunteers.

Chapter 12

Volunteering for Literacy and Education

In This Chapter

✧ What kind of literacy problems there are in the United States

✧ The different kinds of volunteer work you can do for literacy and education

✧ How to decide whether to volunteer for literacy and education

✧ How to find a volunteer opportunity near you

✧ Resource guide for volunteering for literacy and education

You're reading this book, so you probably take reading for granted. Once you've learned to read, few things seem more normal or natural in life. But the sad fact is, millions of people in the United States are functionally illiterate. They can't read well enough to do the simplest of tasks, such as reading a food label or filling out a job application. According to the National Adult Literacy Survey, between 21 and 23 percent of the adult population of the U.S. fall into what the survey calls level 1 of literacy, which means they can't read a food label or a simple story. That means approximately 44 million adults are essentially illiterate in the wealthiest country in the world.

Another 25 to 28 percent—between 45 and 50 million people—fall into level 2, which means they can read some, but lack sufficient reading skills to function successfully in society. All this shows that illiteracy is one of the great hidden problems in the United States.

There's a lot you can do about it, if you want to volunteer. There are many organizations that use volunteers to attack the problem. In this chapter, you'll learn all the ways you can volunteer for literacy and education.

What Types of Literacy Problems Are There?

The term *literacy* refers to whether someone is capable of reading and understanding what is read. There are several literacy problems you'll tackle while volunteering:

✧ **Help children and teens learn to read.** It's sad but true: Many children are never read to while they're growing up. Many don't have parents who are capable of reading, or they have had difficulty learning in school. These are just a few reasons why some children and even teens have a difficult time reading, or can't read at all. As a volunteer, you'll work with children and teens to help them learn to read.

✧ **Help adults learn to read.** Millions of adults lack the skills to read the label on a jar of food or fill out a job application. Some can't read street signs. When you help an adult learn to read, you're helping that adult's children as well, because if parents can read, there's a greater chance their children will read.

It's the Pits

When faced with the thought of helping teach people to read, your first reaction might be, "But I'm not a teacher!" Don't be concerned. Literacy programs will give you training, advice, and books and other materials so that you'll know what you're doing.

✧ **Teach English as a Second Language (ESL).** The United States is a country of immigrants. Almost everyone had ancestors who came here from somewhere else—and the vast majority of those people couldn't speak or read English. Today is no different: Immigrants come into the country not knowing how to read or speak the language. You can help teach people how to read and speak English.

✧ **Teach computer literacy.** In today's world, it's not enough to be able to read. In order to function fully, you need to understand technology and be able to use computers. Increasingly, even the simplest jobs require the use of computers. Unless people are well versed in using computers, they won't be able to get the job they want or function to the fullest of their abilities. Most teens have grown up using computers, and so technology is second nature to them. If this is true for you, you can teach others how to use computers.

What You'll Do as a Volunteer

Now that you've gotten a sense of the kinds of literacy problems our country faces, you're ready to find out what kinds

149

of work you'll do as a volunteer for literacy and education. The truth is, what you'll do is amazingly varied.

There are many different kinds of literacy programs you can volunteer for. There are government-run programs like Head Start, private literacy programs, library-sponsored programs, and other programs that are part public and part private. Here are some of the main things you can expect to do when volunteering:

✧ **Do general work at a library.** Libraries are at the forefront of fighting illiteracy and teaching children and adults how to read. They need help in many ways, doing such things as sorting books that have been returned and putting books back on the shelves.

Inside Scoop

Thousands of children in the United States have parents who are migrant farmworkers. These children can have literacy problems because they may lack access to books. Literacy programs help them. For example, the Pennsylvania Migrant Education program delivers three books each to 6,000 children of migrant farm workers, from ages three and up, every year.

✧ **Read at library story hours.** Libraries generally have story hours during the day for young children. This is a great way to instill the love of reading in children even before they've learned to read. You can volunteer to read during story hours. Not only will you be doing good, you'll be having fun as well!

✧ **Help at summer reading programs.** Most libraries have summer reading programs for children of all ages. Events, games, contests, and other fun activities are often part of these programs. Libraries need help organizing the programs, publicizing them, and running them.

✧ **Teach English as a Second Language (ESL).** Some ESL programs don't let teens teach because they believe that adults don't like to learn from teens. But other programs, such as the Literacy Volunteers of America, freely accept teen volunteers. You'll get a good deal of training before you start. Don't worry if you don't speak a foreign language—when you teach ESL, you'll only speak English and won't use any other language.

✧ **Volunteer for Head Start.** Head Start is a federally run program for preschool-aged children who live in poorer neighborhoods. Its purpose is to prepare children for school. Head Start programs are usually run out of schools or community centers. You probably won't teach in a formal sense at Head Start. Instead, you'll read to the children and help with field trips, simple science experiments, and other activities.

Helping Hands

When I was in college, I volunteered at a neighborhood Head Start. I read to children, helped prepare snacks, and played games with them. It was a great experience—in fact, I think I had as much fun as the kids did! So give it a try. You may find you enjoy it so much, you decide on a career working with children.

✧ **Help with book drives.** Some parents can't afford to buy their children books, so many communities hold book drives in which people donate books. They need volunteers to publicize the drive, gather the books, and help distribute them.

✧ **Tutor at after-school programs.** Many elementary schools have after-school programs in which children are tutored in reading, math, and other subjects. They always need volunteers to help tutor.

✧ **Raise funds.** Literacy programs always need money. Because of that, they frequently hold fund drives and participate in other fund-raising activities. Many volunteers are needed to help with these events.

✧ **Help out around an office.** Literacy programs often need volunteers to help around the office, answering the telephones, filing paperwork, and doing computer work.

✧ **Teach computer skills.** Adults and children who don't have computers at home need help learning basic computer skills. You'll volunteer to help them understand how to use computers and the Internet.

Inside Scoop

How big a program is RIF? Really, *really* big. Think of these numbers: It's given out more than 175 million books, it's in more than 17,000 different communities, and it helps about 3.75 million children every year.

✧ **Volunteer for Reading Is Fundamental (RIF).** One of the most well-known and widespread literacy programs is the Reading Is Fundamental (RIF) program. If you join, you'll tutor children in elementary schools, spend time reading to younger children, donate books, raise funds, and more. It's a very popular program with teen volunteers. A single RIF program in Mesa, Arizona, for example, has about 600 members.

Is Volunteering for Literacy and Education for You?

As you can see, there are a great many kinds of volunteer opportunities available if you want to volunteer for literacy and education. But volunteering in this field isn't for everyone. There are a number of pros and cons to consider.

The Pros of Volunteering for Literacy and Education

Volunteering for literacy and education can be a great experience. Here are all the pros of doing that kind of work:

✧ **It'll help you decide if you want to go into education as a career.** There's no better way to find out whether a career is for you than getting hands-on experience. Volunteering for literacy and education is a great way to get that experience. If you're thinking of going into teaching, becoming a librarian, or a similar career, this is a great way to test it out first.

✧ **It'll help you in your career.** If you do decide to go into education or a related field, your volunteer experience will give you a leg up on other people considering similar work.

✧ **You'll see the immediate results of your work.** When you help teach someone to read, you're not just teaching a skill. You're opening up entire new worlds. You'll get the immediate satisfaction of seeing those worlds open up.

✧ **You'll learn as you teach.** Here's a surprising secret: When you teach, you learn as well. So by helping others learn to read, you'll be helping yourself.

✧ **You'll get to feel like a hero.** Younger children often look up to teens as heroes and role models. When you work one on one with young children, they'll consider you a hero—and that's a great feeling.

✧ **You'll get to meet other teens.** People who volunteer to tutor tend to be friendly and outgoing. You're likely to meet other teens and make new friends.

The Cons of Volunteering for Literacy and Education

Volunteering for literacy and education isn't for everyone. Here are some cons to think about:

✧ **It can cut into your weekends and social life.** Some literacy programs, such as reading to young children, take place on weekends, and so can cut into your social life and take up a good portion of your free time.

✧ **You may be shy and not want to work so closely with others.** Tutoring, reading, and helping with literacy means that you'll be working directly with people or talking to groups. If you're shy; this kind of volunteering may not be for you.

✧ **You may have to give up your study periods.** If you tutor others in school, you'll probably do it during your study periods. That means you'll have to make up that time somewhere else.

✧ **You may be uncomfortable teaching adults.** Some volunteer opportunities require that you teach adults. If that makes you uncomfortable, consider a different type of volunteering for literacy.

Finding a Place to Volunteer Near You

Let's say you've decided that volunteering for literacy and education is for you. Now it's time to find a place to volunteer. The easiest place to start is at your school. It may have a tutoring program where you tutor other teens, so if that's what you want to do, you'll be able to do it right there. Also see if your school has any reading and literacy programs in cooperation with grade schools. Ask if there is a Reading Is Fundamental program, a Literacy Volunteers of America program, or a similar program. Call grade schools and ask if they offer those programs.

Your local library probably offers volunteer opportunities, and has a list of other organizations and groups that need volunteers for literacy. Put the phone book to work, too. Check the Blue Pages, which are the governmental listings in the White Pages. Call the education department in your city or town for a list of volunteer opportunities. Also look in the White Pages under Head Start.

Information Station

A good place to find opportunities to volunteer for literacy is with the Parent Teacher Organization (PTO or PTA) of your school, or of a school near you. These groups are concerned with improving education, so they'll have ideas on how and where you can volunteer to help.

Resource Guide for Volunteering for Literacy and Education

There are many places you can volunteer if you're interested in volunteering for literacy and education. If you're having trouble finding a place near you, check out the following resource guide for help. Here are some of the best organizations to help you find a volunteer opportunity. I've listed the national headquarters of the organizations. Contact the headquarters and let them know you're looking for something in your area.

American Library Association

If you want any kind of information about libraries and literacy, here's the place to go.

50 E. Huron
Chicago, IL 60611
www.ala.org

Laubach Literacy Action

This literacy program helps 175,000 students every year in over 1,000 local organizations.

1320 Jamesville Avenue
Syracuse, NY 13210
315-422-9121
1-888-LAUBACH
www.laubach.org

Literacy Volunteers of America

This programs helps adults as well as their children, and it has volunteering opportunities all across the country.

635 James Street
Syracuse, NY 13203
315-472-0001
www.literacyvolunteers.org

National Head Start Association

This is a national organization made up of the more than 2,000 Head Start organizations around the country.

1651 Prince Street
Alexandria, VA 22314
703-739-0875
www.nhsa.org

National Institute for Literacy

This organization has many programs that use volunteers.

1-800-228-8813
www.nifl.org

Reading Is Fundamental (RIF)

This is perhaps the best organization anywhere for making sure that kids learn to read.

1825 Connecticut Avenue NW
Suite 400
Washington, D.C. 20009
202-287-3196
www.rif.org

The Least You Need to Know

✧ Approximately 44 million adults are functionally illiterate in the United States.

✧ A popular program for volunteering to help children learn to read is Reading Is Fundamental.

✧ Head Start programs are excellent places to volunteer if you want to help young children learn.

✧ You can teach adults English as a Second Language (ESL) even if you don't speak a foreign language, because all the instruction is in English.

✧ Check with your local library, at your school, and at grammar schools to find volunteering opportunities.

157

Chapter 13

Volunteering in Public Safety

In This Chapter

✧ The different kinds of volunteer work available in public safety

✧ What you'll do if you volunteer to help the police, fire department, or emergency medical services (EMS) unit

✧ How to decide if volunteering in public safety is for you

✧ How to find volunteering opportunities in public safety

✧ Resource guide for volunteering in public safety

One of the most satisfying kinds of volunteer work you can do is to help public safety departments—the police, firefighters, and emergency medical services (EMS) units. You'll participate in helping the police do their work, including solving crimes. You'll help firefighters, and even train to fight fires. You may work in ambulances, traveling to the scenes of medical emergencies.

And you'll do it all knowing that you're helping to keep people safe and protect their lives. In this chapter, you'll learn everything you need to know about volunteering in public safety.

What Kind of Work Will You Do?

Becoming a volunteer in public safety is a great way to make sure that your neighborhood and town are as safe as possible, and that people get the help they need in dire emergencies.

In general, there are three areas for volunteers: helping your local police, helping your local fire department, and helping emergency medical services (EMS) units. Here's what you need to know about each before deciding whether to volunteer.

Volunteering at Your Police Department

Most people and teens don't know it, but many local police departments allow teens to volunteer. In fact, not only do they allow it, they encourage it.

The most common way of volunteering at a police department is through a program called Law Enforcement Explorer. This volunteer program, designed for teens, has posts in almost 3,000 towns and cities across the country. An estimated 46,000 teens volunteer in those posts. Each post usually has from three or four to up to 60 teen volunteers, depending on the size of the city or town and how active the police are in accepting volunteers.

To be eligible for the program, you must be between the ages of 14 and 20 and a high school student. You can't have a record of arrest or conviction for a serious offense. Some posts may also have extra eligibility requirements. For example, some may require that you maintain a certain grade point average in school. Your parents or guardians will have to agree to allow you to join the post, and they'll have to sign forms releasing the post from liability if you're hurt in any way when you're volunteering as an Explorer.

Before you can join, you'll be interviewed by one or more people. If you're accepted into the post, you'll receive training, and for the first six months you'll be on probation, which means that for those six months, the post will watch you more closely than normal, to make sure you're doing fine. If you volunteer with no problems, after six months you'll be a permanent member of the post. In addition to your regular volunteering, you'll participate in meetings. These are usually held every week or twice a month, although it can vary from post to post.

Inside Scoop

Some Explorers help gather evidence directly at the scene of crimes, and so help solve crimes. For example, the Glendale Arizona Police note on their Web page that Explorers "work with personnel from the Identification division and collect finger prints, photographs, and respond to major crime scenes to collect evidence."

Explorers do more than just train you and let you know what police do on a daily basis. You actually get to help out the police force as well, and do things such as ride along in cruisers. While what you can do will vary from post to post, here are some of the main things that you'll do:

✧ **Help search for missing people.** At times, people— including children and the elderly—are reported as missing. They may have wandered away from home, gotten lost, or been the victim of a crime. Explorers are part of a group of people who search for the missing person. It's done in an organized way, so that you'll be given maps and clear instructions on what to do.

✧ **Gather criminal evidence.** Sometimes when a crime is committed, evidence can't be found—for example, a gun used in a holdup. Explorers may help gather evidence; for example, to search for a discarded gun.

✧ **Direct traffic and help with crowd control.** Some Explorers may help direct traffic and help with crowd control at special events such as July 4th parades.

✧ **Participate in neighborhood cleanups.** At some Explorer posts, the duties extend beyond policing. Some, for example, sponsor neighborhood cleanup days and programs.

✧ **Teach people about policing.** These days, police do more than investigate crime. They also reach out to the community to teach people how to keep their neighborhoods safe and to protect themselves against crime. You can be part of these programs by doing such things as participating in crime fairs.

✧ **Work as security staff.** At some events, Explorers are used as security officers; for example, at charitable and nonprofit events.

✧ **Ride on police patrol.** Often, Explorers ride along with police officers in patrol cars, getting a firsthand view of what it's like to be a police officer. You must be at least 16 years old and have completed 100 hours of volunteering for the Explorers before you'll be able to do this.

Inside Scoop

When you become an Explorer, you also get an Explorer uniform that you'll wear when volunteering. You may be asked to pay for the uniform, or it might be free. You may also have to pay a low application fee and monthly dues.

Volunteering at Your Fire Department

If you're interested in helping out your local fire department, there's a good chance that you'll be able to find a volunteering opportunity. There are several organizations through which you can volunteer. Just as there is a Law Enforcement Explorer program, there's a Fire Explorer program. Like the Law Enforcement Explorer program, it's run by your local fire department. You must be between the ages of 14 and 20 to be part of the program. You'll learn the basics of firefighting and maintaining fire-fighting equipment as well as help raise funds and educate the public.

Additionally, some fire departments have what they call a junior fire corps, which helps the fire departments in much the same way that Fire Explorers help. If your local fire department allows volunteers, it will probably have one of these programs. It won't, however, have both of them.

It's the Pits

When you volunteer at a local fire department, you may get to use the fire-fighting equipment. Because it's so expensive, some fire departments ask that you leave a deposit on it, which you get back after your volunteering is done. At the Las Vegas Fire Explorer program, for example, you have to leave a $200 deposit. There may also be monthly fees and dues.

The kind of work you'll do will at least partially depend on whether your fire department is a volunteer department or a paid professional department. In general, you'll probably be more involved in the fire department if yours is a volunteer organization. There are several reasons for that. If it's a volunteer organization, it depends solely on volunteers to fight fires, and so can use all the help it can get. Additionally, volunteer departments must always train new firefighters, and a volunteer program for teens is the ideal way to make sure there are new volunteers available. In addition to volunteering, the programs require that you come to regular meetings, which may be weekly, twice a month, or once a month.

Inside Scoop

The United States isn't alone in having teens volunteer for fire departments. In Tokyo, for example, there are 5,000 teen volunteers who work with area fire departments.

No matter which program you join, there are a number of things that you can do if you're interested in volunteering at a local fire department. Here are the most common:

✧ **Help with disaster relief.** Firefighters do more than fight fires. They also frequently help with disaster relief. As a volunteer, you'll help in many ways, and make a real difference in the lives of people in difficult circumstances.

✧ **Learn how to fight fires.** You'll get actual training in how to fight fires—real hands-on experience, not just classroom training. You'll use real fire equipment and participate in mock drills and rescues. In volunteer fire departments, you may be able to participate in putting out small fires (although you won't be involved in larger, dangerous fires). If your town or city has a paid department, though, you won't be able to participate in any firefighting—only volunteer departments will let you do it.

✧ **Help with equipment and firehouse maintenance.** Fire trucks and fire equipment need constant maintenance. They have to always be in tip-top shape so that when a fire alarm comes in, they're ready to go. As a volunteer, you'll help maintain the trucks and equipment. That means everything from cleaning and polishing the trucks to oiling the equipment. You might also help keep the firehouse clean by sweeping the floors.

✧ **Help at the fire scene.** While you won't be allowed to fight dangerous fires, you can still help at the fire scene. You can help set up the staging area—the place where the firefighters set up shop to fight the fire. You can help set up the hoses, make sure that bystanders stay clear, tape the perimeters of the fire scene, and other tasks.

✧ **Raise funds.** Volunteer fire departments in particular always need money and regularly hold many different kinds of fundraisers. As a volunteer, you'll be a vital part of fund-raising efforts.

✧ **Help out at special events.** Often, firefighters are called on to assist at a variety of special events. For example, in many towns the local fire department is in charge of the July 4th fireworks display, or at least is nearby in case there are any problems.

✧ **Help with outreach and education.** Fire departments do more than just put out fires. They also educate people about fire safety, so that fewer fires are started and people know what to do if they're caught in a fire. You'll help during Fire Prevention Week, as well as in other kinds of community involvement.

✧ **Learn first aid.** Firefighters need to know first aid and what to do in the case of medical emergencies, so you'll learn those skills as well.

165

Volunteering with Emergency Medical Services (EMS) Units

If you're interested in public safety, one of the most satisfying ways you can help others is to volunteer with an emergency medical services (EMS) unit—in other words, ambulances and similar rescue services.

Not all communities allow teen volunteers to help these units. Just as some towns have volunteer fire departments, some have volunteer EMS units. Other towns and cities have paid ones. You're more likely to be able to volunteer with a volunteer EMS unit than a paid one. The laws and rules about who can and can't work in an EMS unit vary from state to state and town to town. Some states let you volunteer in a unit if you're 14 years old or older; in other states you must be 16 years old or older. In others, you must be at least 18 or 21. It's easy to find out what the rules are for your area—make a call and ask. They'll tell you whether there's a volunteer program and if there are any age limits.

The most widespread program for volunteering for EMS units is the EMS Explorer program. If your town has a volunteer fire department, it probably has a volunteer EMS unit as well. Often, in those cases, the fire and EMS Explorer posts are often combined, with one post serving both functions.

Helping Hands

Explorer programs for police, firefighting, and emergency medical services all got their start through the Boy Scouts Explorer program. But you don't need to join the Boy Scouts in order to be an Explorer. And you don't need to be a boy, either—Explorer programs are open to both males and females.

When you volunteer to help an EMS unit, you're helping to save lives. These units respond to medical emergencies and rescues, rushing people to the hospital as well as providing potentially life-saving care at the scene.

If you live in an area that accepts EMS volunteers, you'll probably be welcomed with open arms. You'll be trained in things such as cardiopulmonary resuscitation or CPR (restoring breathing and a heartbeat to someone whose heart has stopped beating or who has stopped breathing). You'll also get training for things such as basic life support—things you need to know in medical emergencies.

You may also get certified as a medical response technician (MRT) or emergency medical technician (EMT). When you're certified, you'll be able to help at the scenes of emergencies. An EMT is more advanced than an MRT. There may be age limits on when you can be certified for these things.

EMS Explorers and similar volunteers do a variety of things when working for EMS units. Here are the most common tasks:

✧ **Help in medical emergencies.** If you've been certified as an EMT or MRT, you can help by directing what needs to be done at the scene of an emergency.

✧ **Help with radio communications.** This means taking phone calls, and communicating with ambulances, as well as caring for the equipment and making sure it's in working order.

✧ **Drive an ambulance.** Depending on your age, training, and the laws where you live, you may drive an ambulance to and from the scene of the emergency. You'll need special training and certification to do this.

✧ **Provide miscellaneous help.** Ambulances and equipment need to be maintained; you can help do that. And there are always miscellaneous tasks that need doing.

✧ **Raise funds.** Fund-raising is absolutely vital, especially if you live in an area with a volunteer EMS unit. You'll help out at fund drives and similar programs.

✧ **Help with public education.** EMS units do more than respond to emergencies. They educate people about public safety—and they always need volunteers willing to lend a hand.

Inside Scoop

One benefit of volunteering at an EMS unit—as well as with fire and police departments—is that frequently, they offer college scholarships to those teens who volunteer for them. Not every volunteer gets a scholarship, but if you volunteer, you'll be eligible for scholarships that nonvolunteers can't get.

Is Volunteering for Public Safety for You?

As you can see, there are a great many kinds of volunteer opportunities available to you if you want to volunteer in public safety. But working in this field isn't for everyone. There are some pros and cons to consider.

The Pros of Volunteering in Public Safety

Volunteering in public safety can be a great experience. In fact, for some people, it can be life-transforming. Here are all the pros of doing that kind of volunteering:

✧ **It will give you a leg up on a career in public safety.** There's nothing like real-life experience in public safety to help you decide if the field is for you. You can save a

lot of time by volunteering first. The Redding, California, Law Enforcement Explorer program did a survey
and found that from 10 to 15 percent of teens who
were Explorers went on to become full-time police officers in the state of California. It's also a great way to
start a career in firefighting or with an EMS unit.

✧ **It will help you get into college and get a job.**
Volunteering in public safety is an excellent qualifica-
tion on a resume or college application. Some programs
will also qualify you for special college scholarships.

✧ **You'll gain an enormous sense of satisfaction.** Can
anything be more satisfying than knowing you've
helped keep people safe and possibly saved lives?
Probably not. You'll find it enormously satisfying.

✧ **You'll get a great education.** You'll learn things such
as the inner workings of a police department, how to
fight fires, and how to treat people in medical emergencies.

The Cons of Volunteering in Public Safety

Volunteering in public safety isn't for everyone. It can be a
very difficult kind of volunteering. Here are some cons to
consider:

✧ **It can be dangerous.** You'll be near fires, at accident
and crime scenes, involved in crowd control, as well as
other kinds of things that might not be safe. So think
seriously about whether you want to expose yourself to
dangers. The dangers are small, but they're still there.

✧ **It can be expensive.** Depending on the program you
join, you may have to pay for your own uniform and
equipment, as well as pay a membership fee and dues.

✧ **It can be incredibly demanding.** Fires and medical
emergencies don't occur when you happen to have free
time. Depending on how you volunteer, you may have
to be constantly on call, eating into your free time.

✧ **You may face very difficult and unpleasant situations.** At accidents, medical emergencies, and fires you'll come across severely injured people and people in extreme physical and emotional distress. If you can't handle those kinds of situations, volunteering in public safety isn't for you.

✧ **It involves a regular commitment of time.** If you become an Explorer, you must promise to attend regular meetings, in addition to any other volunteer work you might do. If your schedule doesn't allow this kind of commitment, consider other kinds of volunteer work.

It's the Pits

Have you ever been in trouble with the law for something other than a parking ticket? If so, you might have a difficult time volunteering for public safety. Some departments stipulate that anyone who has had a brush with the law is not allowed to do volunteer work.

Finding a Place to Volunteer Near You

It's easy to find volunteering opportunities for the police, fire department, and EMS units. Simply call them up. There's no need to look for any national or statewide organizations, because they really won't be able to help.

Look in your local telephone book for the phone numbers. Check the Blue Pages, which is the part of the phone book that has telephone numbers for local governments. Don't call the emergency 911 number—those are for emergencies only, not for routine phone calls. When you call, explain that you want to volunteer, and ask who you can talk to.

Resource Guide for Volunteering in Public Safety

If you want to volunteer in public safety, first check out your local police and fire department or EMS unit. There really aren't any national organizations that can help beyond that. But if you want more information about volunteering in public safety, check out these resources.

Fire and Emergency Medical Services (EMS) Explorers

This excellent Web site gives you the rundown on what Fire and EMS Explorers do. It offers advice on how to become one, and lists all the scholarships open to Fire and EMS Explorers.

www.learning-for-life.org/exploring/fire/index.html

Law Enforcement Explorers

This excellent Web site gives you the rundown on what Law Enforcement Explorers do. It offers advice on how to become one, and lists all the scholarships open to Law Enforcement Explorers.

www.learning-for-life.org/exploring/lawenforcement/main.html

Learning for Life

This group oversees many of the Explorer programs in fire, police, and EMS units, so it's a great resource for finding information about all of these programs. If you can't find an Explorers opportunity near you, contact them.

1325 West Walnut Hill Lane
P.O. Box 152079
Irving, TX 75015-2079
972-580-2000
www.learning-for-life.org

171

The Least You Need to Know

✧ When you volunteer for your local police department, you'll do everything from educating the public to gathering evidence at crime scenes.

✧ The Explorers program helps teens volunteer in police departments, fire departments, and at EMS units.

✧ To volunteer for public safety, you must be at least 14 years old, and in some instances 16 years old or older.

✧ If your fire department or EMS is a volunteer department, there's a greater chance they'll accept volunteers than if it's staffed by paid professionals.

✧ Often, Explorer posts for fire departments and EMS units are combined.

✧ While the work can be demanding and even dangerous, there is no greater satisfaction than knowing you've helped people and perhaps saved lives.

Part 4

Beyond Volunteering

If you get really serious about volunteering, I'll tell you how you can create your own volunteering opportunity so that you don't need to rely on an organization. You'll also learn how to find overseas volunteer opportunities, how you can volunteer full-time for a year and even get scholarship money, and what to consider if you're thinking of going into social work or working for a nonprofit institution as a career.

Chapter 14

Creating Your Own Volunteering Experience

In This Chapter

✧ Why you might want to create a solo volunteering opportunity

✧ Is solo volunteering right for you?

✧ How you can create a solo volunteering experience

✧ Creating your own solo volunteering network

So far in this book, you're learned about all the different kinds of volunteering you can do to help others by joining a group. For the vast majority of people, that's the best way to volunteer. Volunteering isn't always an easy thing to do, and to do it, you need support, organization, resources, money, and time. Well-run, organized groups provide much of that for you and more. They also know about all the different volunteer opportunities available.

But that doesn't mean you *have* to join a group in order to volunteer. You can go solo and do volunteering on your own. Many other people have done it and have done it well. One person on his or her own *can* make a big difference in the community and in the world.

In this chapter, I'll tell you what kind of opportunities there are for solo volunteering and help you decide whether solo volunteering is right for you. You'll also learn how to build your own solo volunteering opportunity.

Yes, You Can Go It Alone

There are many different ways to go it alone as a volunteer. It can be as simple as creating your own fund-raiser for a favorite charity or group, or as complicated as starting an entirely new volunteer organization on your own. Later in this chapter, I'll give you some ideas on how to create your own volunteering experience.

Inside Scoop

My brother Eliot was always helping others. In college, he built a food cart and sold organic foods during lunchtime as an alternative to cafeteria food. Every penny of profit was donated to feed the hungry. He ended up organizing a group of friends to buy the food, make the lunches, and sell them, so his solo experience wasn't solo for long!

Why bother to go solo? There are many reasons why you might want to volunteer on your own rather than join an organized group. Here are some of the main reasons why you might want to create your own volunteering experience:

✧ **There are no suitable volunteering opportunities where you live.** You may live in an area that has few volunteering opportunities. Or perhaps the opportunities that do exist aren't suitable for you. That doesn't mean that you can't volunteer—it just means you should consider creating your own volunteering experience.

✧ **You don't have time for a regularly scheduled volunteering job.** Most volunteering opportunities require that you show up at a certain time for certain days of the week for a certain amount of time. It might be that your schedule doesn't permit that kind of regular volunteering, or that you don't want to have to volunteer on a regular schedule.

✧ **You want to try things on your own.** There are some people who need independence and prefer to try things on their own. If you're one of those people, going solo may well be for you.

Questions to Ask Yourself Before Going It Alone

To help you decide whether you should go volunteer solo, ask yourself these questions. Your answers will help you decide whether you should design your own volunteering experience or work with an existing group:

✧ **Do you have enough confidence in your abilities to go it alone?** If you don't, it's best to stick with a group.

✧ **Do you enjoy working by yourself and being in control?** If so, then going solo might be right for you. If not, don't try to do it by yourself.

✧ **Do you have an abundance of energy?** You'll need it if you're going to design your own volunteering plan.

✧ **Do you have enough optimism to see it through the hard times?** Since you won't be able to rely on others, you'll need to have a great deal of optimism, and the ability to stick to the plan even when things don't go exactly the way that you had hoped.

How to Create a Solo Volunteering Experience

Let's say that you've decided that going solo is for you—you want to create your own volunteering experience. Now what? If you're independent and creative enough, it isn't that hard to create your own volunteering experience. Here's how to do it:

✧ **Choose an issue.** What issue in your community or in the greater world most concerns you? Hunger? Illiteracy? Animal welfare? Thing big, not small. At this point, you're merely brainstorming. Once you begin to put your ideas into effect, you can start to narrow them down to manageable things that you can do on your own. Once you decide on the issue you'd like to pursue, you're ready to begin creating your volunteering opportunity.

✧ **Make sure the issue matches your interests.** When you go solo, you're going to pour a lot of yourself into your volunteering. So make sure that the issue you choose matches your interests and is one that you really care about.

Information Station

To get help deciding what issue concerns you most, go back through Part 3, Finding Volunteering Experiences." It's a comprehensive guide to the different problems that volunteers can help solve.

✧ **Research the issue.** Before you can put a plan together, you need to learn as much as you can about the issue. Use the library and the Internet to start off. Check with your local librarian. Using the resources in this book, find out whether there are already volunteer organizations that tackle the problem you're interested in. Then contact them to find out more information about the issue, and to see if they have any ideas on what you might do on your own.

✧ **Design a plan.** Once you know the problem, start brainstorming some solutions. Bounce ideas off your parents and friends. Come up with as many solutions as possible, then cut it down from there.

✧ **Gather the resources you need.** Will you require money? If so, how will you get it—by fund-raising or some other method? Can you hook into existing volunteer, private, and governmental groups to get their help? Will you need to recruit other people or can you do everything by yourself? What kind of publicity will you need?

✧ **Put your plan into effect.** It's time to go full-steam ahead. Make sure along the way that you gauge the effectiveness of what you're doing so that you can make any changes.

Helping Hands

Solo volunteering need not involve a long-term commitment. If you can only give a day or a few hours, it's still worth doing. In that amount of time, you can make a difference by doing things such as collecting money for a nonprofit organization that helps the poor.

Some Sample Solo Volunteering Opportunities

While there are many kinds of solo volunteering opportunities you can dream up, here are some ideas to get you started:

✧ **Make gift boxes for the holidays.** People who are in institutions such as hospitals and nursing homes often feel cut off from the world, and this is especially painful during holidays. Make gift boxes and deliver them to these folks during the holidays. (Steer clear of including food items in the basket if you don't know a person's diet; you might include something the person is not allowed to have.) You might want to include in your gift baskets greeting cards, stuffed animals, silk plants or flowers, pictures, playing cards, and similar items.

✧ **Start a donation drive.** Many organizations desperately need donations, and not just of money. Shelters, for example, need donations of canned food and other goods. Programs like Toys for Tots needs donations of new toys. You can start a donation drive of your own simply by asking for donations in your neighborhood or in your parent's place of work.

✧ **Organize a neighborhood cleanup day.** Is your neighborhood or another neighborhood in need of a cleanup? No need to wait for an organization to do it for you— take control and organize it yourself. Get your friends and neighbors together and organize a cleanup day.

✧ **Create an oral history project.** Seniors have had a lifetime of stories to tell and often no one to listen to them. Go to senior centers and interview the residents, and then type their stories on your computer, print them out, and bind them into a book to give to the seniors.

✧ **Collect food and supplies for an animal shelter.**
Animal shelters are often short of money, so they can
always use donations, especially of pet food and supplies like blankets and towels. You can organize a drive
to collect these supplies and donate them to a shelter.

Creating Your Own Volunteering Network

Working solo can be a great experience. But it can get lonely,
and it can be difficult working alone without other people's
help and input. To help face those problems, you should create your own volunteering network. You'll want to have contact with a group of people who can help you when you
need something—something as simple as someone to talk to
or as difficult as figuring out how to raise money.

It's not that hard to find your own network of people for
this. For a start, research what organizations do the kind of
work that you'll be doing solo. Call those organizations and
ask who you can talk to when you need help or ideas.

Local librarians are always full of resources and ideas. When
you go to the library for help, always try to go to the same
librarian. Very soon you'll have a friend who can offer ideas
and aid. Turn to your parents, teachers, friends, and guidance
counselors as well.

Keep in touch with people in your network regularly, even if
only to say hello and let them know what you've been doing.
E-mail is a great way to do this. You might even design a
simple newsletter that you send out to your network on a
monthly basis. You can also create your own Web site where
you report on your doings. It's easy to do. Go to a site like
GeoCities at www.geocities.com. It lets you create your own
Web site for free, and gives you the tools to build your own
site, even if you've never built one before.

The Least You Need to Know

◇ If there are no suitable volunteering experiences near you, or if you have scheduling problems with those that do exist, you might want to try solo volunteering.

◇ When you do solo volunteering, you'll have independence and the satisfaction of knowing the work you did was created only by you.

◇ To avoid burnout, it's a good idea to build up a network of people you can talk to and from whom you can get ideas and support.

◇ Make sure that your solo volunteering is something the community needs and that holds a great deal of interest for you.

Chapter 15

Getting Serious About Helping Others

In This Chapter

✧ Considering a career in social work or with a nonprofit organization

✧ The pros and cons of going into social work and working for nonprofit institutions

✧ Top questions you should ask yourself before going into social work or working for a nonprofit institution

✧ How you can pursue a career in social work or with a nonprofit institution

✧ Devoting a year of your life to helping others with AmeriCorps

✧ Finding overseas volunteer experiences

As I've mentioned throughout this book, volunteering can be a great experience. You may like it so much that you'd like to do more than volunteer occasionally. There's a lot you can do if you want to get more serious about volunteering. You can make it your career, and after high school or college work full-time for nonprofit organizations or in social work. If you're not sure you want it as your career, but want to do more than occasional volunteering, you can spend a year of your life volunteering to help others—and get nearly $5,000 for college—in the AmeriCorps program. And if you'd like to volunteer overseas, there are many amazing opportunities for you.

So if you're interested in getting more serious about volunteering, read on. You'll be amazed at all the different ways you can help others, while getting the most out of your own life.

Should You Devote Yourself to Social Work?

For many people, volunteering is one of the great experiences of their lives—and they continue to volunteer well beyond their teens and throughout their lives. But if you want to help others, you don't have to make it a sideline to your life, something you do in your spare time or once a year during the holidays. There are many, many ways to make a living helping others.

Think of all the types of organizations mentioned in this book. They need full-time employees to help run those businesses. That means thousands and thousands of jobs. How many? No one really knows. But in their book *Jobs and Careers with Nonprofit Organizations: Profitable Opportunities with Nonprofits* (see Appendix B, "Books About Volunteering"), Ron and Caryl Krannich claim that there are one million nonprofit institutions in the United States that spend $50 billion annually, and employ nearly 10 million people. And that doesn't even include the countless government jobs that are available, such as teachers and social workers.

No matter how you add it up, if you're interested in helping others for a living, there's a job waiting for you.

Rather than detail all the different kinds of jobs at nonprofit institutions that are available, I'll simply point you back through the rest of this book. Take a look through all the chapters. That details for you the kinds of work you can do for nonprofit institutions. From helping the needy, to aiding animals, working in the arts, fighting hunger, to devoting yourself to education, there are countless ways you can make a living helping others.

But is working for nonprofit institutions or in social work for you? The simplest way to find out is to start volunteering, of course. Volunteer in more than one kind of field, and with more than one kind of organization in that field. That'll give you a good head start on figuring out whether it's right for you.

You should also consider the pros and cons of working for nonprofits or in social work. That's what we'll go over in the next section.

The Pros of Working for Nonprofit Institutions or in Social Work

There are many good reasons to work for a nonprofit institution or in social work. Here are some of the main ones:

✧ **You'll know you're helping others.** It's an incredible opportunity to make a living while helping others. You'll be able to do good while making money.

✧ **You'll achieve a high level of satisfaction.** Very few things in life are as rewarding as helping others. If you do it for a living, you'll get those rewards every day, not just on an occasional basis.

✧ **The work is often exciting.** In this kind of work, you won't be stuck in a typical office job, watching the clock. The work changes constantly, every day is different, and there's a palpable sense of excitement to what you do. Very few jobs in the world are like that.

✧ **The workplace is supportive.** Nonprofit institutions tend not to be infected with the dog-eat-dog atmosphere that can be found at many corporations.

✧ **It's often easy to break in.** It's usually not difficult to get an entry-level job at a nonprofit or similar institution, so you may not face an exhausting job search.

✧ **It's easy to try out.** A simple way to try out this kind of career is to volunteer first, so you'll have lost nothing when you try it out—and you'll also do good by helping others.

✧ **It can be a good career move.** There are many nonprofits out there, and you can ultimately make a good living working for them. But even if you decide to move on, working for a nonprofit institution is excellent training for other kinds of work. It impresses would-be employers as well.

Information Station

Good Works: A Guide To Careers in Social Change, edited by Donna Colvin and Ralph Nader and published in 1994, is an excellent book for anyone interested in nonprofit work. Order it from Essential Information, P.O. Box 19405, Washington, D.C. 20036.

The Cons of Working for Nonprofit Institutions or in Social Work

While doing good works is a great and satisfying full-time profession, it's not for everyone. Here are some of the main drawbacks:

✧ **The pay is usually not that good.** While there are exceptions, generally the pay at nonprofit institutions is less than you'd receive at other jobs. Don't be surprised to see salaries that are 25 percent (or more, in some cases) less than what you'd get at another job.

✧ **If you want to advance, you may have to hop from job to job.** Many nonprofit institutions are small, and because of that, there isn't always a lot of opportunity for career advancement. That means to get more challenging and rewarding jobs, you may have to jump from nonprofit institution to nonprofit institution.

✧ **Many nonprofits face uncertain futures.** Often, nonprofit organizations depend on fund-raising for their financial viability. An unsuccessful fund-raising year can mean bad news for an organization—and for the people who work there.

Helping Hands

If you're still not sure whether you want to work for a nonprofit institution, try one of the several groups that let you work full-time as a volunteer right after high school or college. You'll find out more about these organizations later in this chapter.

✧ **It can be easy to burn out.** It's easy to burn yourself out working at nonprofit institutions. Low pay, long hours, and the difficulties of trying to help others in the face of an often uncaring world can be a recipe for burnout.

✧ **You may have to work long hours.** Very often, nonprofit institutions require that you work long hours. If you're not willing to devote yourself to your work to that degree, this kind of work isn't for you.

Some Questions to Ask Yourself

You've learned the pros and cons of working for nonprofit institutions or in social work. But if you're still not sure whether it's a career for you, ask yourself these questions:

✧ **How important is money to you?** If you work at nonprofit institutions, you won't get rich. If money is important to you, you shouldn't go into the field.

✧ **How important is the sense that you're doing good?** Do you need to feel that the work you're doing is vital and doing good in the world? If the answer is yes, then this is a field for you.

✧ **How well do you work with others?** When you work at nonprofits, you'll inevitably work very closely with many diverse people and as a part of one or more teams. If you're a loner, this work probably isn't your cup of tea.

✧ **Are you a communicator?** Above all, this field requires the ability to communicate well with others, and to be comfortable communicating. If you're good at it, that's great; if it's difficult for you, you may be in for a bit of trouble.

✧ **Do you like working for small, friendly organizations?** Many, but not all, nonprofit organizations are small. Very often, small organizations are "friendlier" than larger ones—everyone tends to know one another, and there is less red tape and bureaucracy. If this appeals to you, then it's a plus. If not, it could mean trouble.

✧ **How comfortable are you raising money?** Fact of life: Most nonprofit institutions spend a good deal of their time raising money. This means planning and participating in a wide variety of fund-raising drives and events. If you're not comfortable doing this, you may run into difficulty.

Inside Scoop

If you're interested in social work, you'll find that many jobs are found at local, state, and federal government agencies rather than in nonprofit organizations. So if you're thinking of going into social work, keep in mind that you could end up working for the government.

Pursuing a Career in Social Work or with Nonprofit Institutions

You've looked at the pros and cons, and you've asked yourself the questions. You've decided that yes, a career in social work or with a nonprofit institution is for you. Now it's time to start planning for your career. You're a teen, so your career is still years away. However, there are things you can do right now to help prepare yourself for that career:

✧ **Volunteer in as many places as possible.** Start today, and volunteer in as many different kinds of places as you possibly can. Volunteering at one place won't give you the widest exposure to the field possible. Also, volunteering at several places will be helpful on your resume. Don't volunteer at more than one place at a time, though. Instead, volunteer at one place, and then another. But give each place a fair shot, six months or so, so that you'll get a feel for what it's like to work there.

✧ **Start networking.** Frequently when people are hired for jobs, it isn't through the classifieds or help-wanted ads. It's often through knowing people, who may tell you a job is open. The way you'll find out about those openings is by knowing as many people in the field as possible.

Information Station

For help in finding a nonprofit job, check out the Nonprofit Career Network at www.nonprofitcareer.com. You'll find a job resource center, a comprehensive directory of nonprofit organizations, information about nonprofit job fairs, and more. You can also go to www.essential.org/goodworks and search for nonprofit jobs near you.

✧ **Get letters of recommendation.** Letters of recommendation impress potential employers. At each of your volunteer opportunities, ask someone for a letter of recommendation. Put them in a safe place for when you need them.

✧ **"Shadow" a nonprofit employee.** The best way to find out what it's like to work at a nonprofit institution is to spend a day with an employee there. Ask if you can spend the day watching what he or she does.

✧ **Practice writing your resume.** It's never too soon to start writing a resumé. Using the tips and advice I offer in Chapter 4, "Getting Your Dream Volunteering Job," put together your resumé. Write it with an eye toward getting a full-time job, not just a volunteer opportunity.

✧ **Apply to the right college.** What kind of nonprofit work or social work do you want to do? Are you interested in the environment? In teaching? In working with animals? In helping the homeless? Many colleges have programs designed for specific nonprofit works. Check with your guidance counselor. He or she will know what colleges have the right programs.

Helping Hands

A great way to know what nonprofit jobs require in terms of skills and experience is to look at the job listings. They'll detail exactly what's needed. A great place on the Web to find job listings for nonprofits is at www.nonprofitjobs.org.

AmeriCorps and Beyond: Full-Time Volunteering Experiences

You're still in high school, so you may think that working to help the needy and in a nonprofit institution is many years away. Well, here's news for you: You don't have to wait. There's an excellent government-backed program that lets people from ages 17 to 24 work full-time as volunteers. For your work, you'll receive a living allowance, and depending on where you volunteer, possibly housing as well. (In any event, the living allowance will be enough to cover food and housing.) You'll also receive an education award of $4,725 that you can use toward college.

The program is called AmeriCorps, and it's great for anyone serious about volunteering. It's often called the "domestic Peace Corps" because in many ways it's like the Peace Corps, in which college graduates volunteer to work overseas. But at AmeriCorps, you work in the United States, and you can be as young as 17 years old in order to volunteer.

You'll be able to work at any one of numerous excellent volunteer programs, such as the American Red Cross, Habitat for Humanity, local community centers, churches and synagogues, and Boys and Girls Clubs. You can tutor; assist crime victims; turn vacant lots into neighborhood parks; restore coastlines; help the needy, elderly, and homeless; respond to natural disasters; and much, much more. In fact, you'll be able to choose from almost 1,000 national and local groups. You'll receive extensive training, both at the beginning of the program and during the course of the program.

If you volunteer, you'll be far from alone. Some 40,000 people volunteer through AmeriCorps every year. What's great about the program is that it's not a big, federal bureaucracy. Instead, you'll volunteer at a local organization.

You'll work for 10 months to a year if you join the program, depending on which local organization you choose to work for. You'll need to fill out an application form in which you list your education and any employment experience you've had, and provide a statement describing why you want to join. You'll also have to get two people (they can't be relatives) to fill out a brief reference form.

That's all it takes. For more information and an application, go to www.americorps.org or call 1-800-942-2677. You can also talk directly to an AmeriCorps recruiter—someone who lives in your state who can give you information about AmeriCorps. To find a local recruiter, call AmeriCorps at the number above or head to www://americorps.org/joining/findrecruiter.html.

Information Station

One of AmeriCorps' best and most innovative programs is called City Year, in which you volunteer for a year to help revitalize city neighborhoods. The work ranges from running after-school programs and urban summer camps to working to prevent domestic violence. For details, contact City Year at 285 Columbus Avenue, 5th floor, Boston, MA 02116; 617-927-2500; www.cityyear.org.

Finding Overseas Volunteer Experiences

If you're interested in volunteering to help others, you don't need to feel confined to the United States. There's a whole world out there, and many jobs that need doing. You can help stamp out hunger, provide medical assistance, improve agriculture, help people develop economic self-sufficiency, prevent blindness, stop environmental degradation, and many, many more much-needed jobs.

You don't have to wait until you graduate from college to find an overseas volunteer experience. Until you're older, you'll have to do it as a volunteer instead of as a full-time job, but still, there are overseas volunteer experiences waiting for you. In general, these opportunities are held during the summer, when you have weeks or months free so that you can get the most out of volunteering overseas.

If you do volunteer to help overseas, keep in mind that you might have to spend some of your own money. Since most of these organizations don't have extra cash, you'll probably have to pay for transportation yourself. And you'll probably have to pay for your own living expenses. But because the volunteer opportunities typically are in the poorer countries of the world, living expenses tend to be minimal.

How do you find an overseas volunteer opportunity? A good clearinghouse is the U.S. Agency for International Development (USAID). USAID is the primary government program that helps other countries escape from poverty, provides disaster relief to other countries, and encourages other countries to engage in democratic reforms. Head to their Web site at www.usaid.org for all the information you'll need about the organization. It also includes helpful information and links to overseas volunteer organizations.

USAID also has volunteer positions available, although it doesn't have a large number of them. To qualify, you must be at least 16 years old, a U.S. citizen, in school, and have a grade point average of at least 3.0 out of 4.0. For details, go to www.usaid.gov/educ_training/scholarship.html.

Another excellent place to turn is Volunteers for Peace (VFP). This innovative program sponsors "workcamps" in many other countries. You'll work from two to three weeks in places such as Armenia, Estonia, France, and Germany. In addition to transportation, you'll pay between $200 to $300 for room and board. You'll help rebuild nations that are suffering the after-effects of earthquakes, work at a children's hospital, help in an orphanage, and similar work. For information, contact VFP at 1034 Tiffany Road, Belmont, VT 05730; 802-259-2759; www.vfp.org.

It's the Pits

Before agreeing to volunteer overseas, do some research at your local library and read the newspapers to find out as much as you can about the country where you've going to volunteer. Not every place is as safe as the United States, and you don't want to end up in an area where there is terrorism or dangerous diseases.

The Amigos de Las Americas program is another excellent way to volunteer to provide public health services throughout Latin America. You'll volunteer in countries such as Honduras, Mexico, Brazil, Costa Rica, and Bolivia, doing such things as building houses and stoves for the needy, planting trees, and teaching residents about public health. For information, contact Amigos de Las Americas at 5618 Star Lane, Houston, TX 77057; 1-800-231-7796; www.amigoslink.org.

The Least You Need to Know

✧ A career in social work or with a nonprofit institution is satisfying because you'll be helping others, and tends to be exciting work in a creative, stimulating environment.

✧ If you're thinking of going into social work or working for a nonprofit institution, volunteer at as many places as possible, network with as many people as possible, and ask your guidance counselor for the best colleges to which you should apply.

✧ If you're interested in spending a year helping others and in getting nearly $5,000 for college, join the AmeriCorps program. For details, go to www.americorps.com.

✧ There are many volunteer opportunities available overseas, primarily in the summer. You may have to pay for your own transportation and living expenses.

Resource Guide for Teen Volunteers

No matter what kind of volunteering you want to do, you'll be able to find resources to help you in this appendix. From volunteering in hospitals to pet shelters, for the needy and beyond, you'll find a resource for you.

Note that I've listed the national headquarters of the organizations. Contact the headquarters and let them know you're looking for something in your area.

General Volunteering Resources

If you're looking for general resources on volunteering, or groups that can help with several different kinds of volunteering, here's where to go.

AIDS Action

This group is a network of 3,200 national AIDS service organizations. If you're looking to volunteer at an AIDS organization, it's a great place to start.

1906 Sunderland Place NW
Washington, D.C. 20036
www.aidsaction.org

American Cancer Society

This group is the main organization for leading the fight against cancer through fund-raising, public education, and lobbying the government.

1599 Clifton Road NE
Atlanta, GA 30329
1-800-ACS-2345 or 404-320-3333
www.cancer.org

American Council of the Blind

This group helps the blind in many ways, and has state and regional groups associated with it. It uses many volunteers and always needs help.

1155 15th Street NW
Suite 1004
Washington, D.C. 20005
1-800-424-8666 or 202-467-5081
www.acb.org

American Heart Association

This organization is the primary organization for fighting heart disease and stroke. It does a great deal of fund-raising and public education.

7272 Greenville Avenue
Dallas, TX 75231
214-373-6300
www.americanheart.org

American Lung Association

The American Lung Association works to prevent lung disease and promotes lung health. There are local chapters across the country.

1740 Broadway
New York, NY 10019
212-315-8700
www.lungusa.org

American Medical Association

The American Medical Association is the country's largest organization of doctors. It's a great clearinghouse for finding out any information about medicine, and so will be helpful in finding volunteer opportunities.

515 North State Street
Chicago, IL 60610
312-464-5000
www.ama-assn.org

American Public Health Association

State public health associations do a great deal of public education and are great places to volunteer. They're also great places to help you find places to volunteer.

800 I Street NW
Washington, D.C. 20001
202-777-APHA
www.apha.org

American Red Cross

The American Red Cross helps victims of disasters such as hurricanes, collects half the nation's blood supply through donations, and teaches cardiopulmonary resuscitation CPR), among many other jobs. It uses many, many volunteers in many different ways. There's a Red Cross near you. if you can't find it, check the Red Cross's national association.

431 18th Street NW
Washington, D.C. 20006
202-639-3520
www.redcross.org

Campaign for Tobacco-Free Kids

This group works to stamp out smoking among kids and teens. A lot of the work is done by kid and teen volunteers.

1707 L Street NW
Suite 800
Washington, D.C. 20036
202-296-5469
www.tobaccofreekids.org

Idealist

This Web site is an excellent resource for finding volunteering opportunities near you or in other parts of the country.

www.idealist.org

Landmark Volunteers

This group helps find high school students volunteer opportunities for two weeks during the summer at one of several historical, cultural, environmental, or social service institutions.

P.O. Box 455
Sheffield, MA 01257
413-229-0255
www.volunteers.com

March of Dimes

The March of Dimes fights birth defects and has many different kinds of well-established volunteer organizations.

1275 Mamaroneck Avenue
White Plains, NY 10605
1-888-663-4637
www.modimes.org

Special Olympics

The Special Olympics provide sports training and athletic competition in a variety of Olympic-style sports for people with mental handicaps. The organization relies very heavily on volunteers. If you can't track down your local branch, contact the main office.

1325 G Street NW
Suite 500
Washington, D.C. 20005
202-628-3630
www.specialolympics.org

Volunteers of America

This national program runs many local human service programs that help people in need. It's also a great resource for getting solo volunteering ideas. Make sure to read the group's newsletter, available for free on its Web site.

1660 Duke Street
Alexandria, VA 22314
703-341-5000
www.voa.org

Volunteer Match

This is a great Web site that will match you up with volunteer opportunities. You say what your interests are and where you want to volunteer and the site does the rest.

www.volunteermatch.org

Medical Volunteers Resources

Here are some of the best organizations you'll find to help you find a volunteer opportunity if you want to be a medical volunteer.

Volunteering for the Needy in Shelters, for the Hungry, or with the Elderly

Here are some of the best organizations you'll find to help you find a volunteer opportunity if you're interested in working in shelters, for the hungry, or with the elderly.

Alliance for Families and Children

The Alliance for Families and Children is made up of 350 organizations that help children and families. It helps over five million people in more than 2,000 communities, so it's a great place for finding volunteer experiences for helping the needy. Contact the central organization for information about how to find volunteering opportunities in your area.

11700 W. Lake Park Drive
Milwaukee, WI 53224
1-800-221-3726
www.alliance1.org

American Association of Retired People (AARP)

The AARP is the country's largest organization for people 50 years old and older. It's also a great place for finding out about volunteering to help seniors. There are many AARP chapters that can help you find a volunteering experience, or you can contact the national offices.

601 E Street NW
Washington, D.C. 20049
1-800-424-3410
www.aarp.org

American Red Cross

The American Red Cross helps provide shelter for victims of disasters such as floods and hurricanes. There's a Red Cross near you. If you can't find it, check the Red Cross's national association.

431 18th Street NW
Washington, D.C. 20006
202-639-3520
www.redcross.org

Meals on Wheels Association of America

Meals on Wheels are local organizations that deliver hot meals to seniors in communities across the country. To find a branch near you, check the national headquarters.

1-800-677-1116
www.projectmeal.org

National Coalition for the Homeless

The National Coalition for the Homeless is devoted to helping the homeless in a variety of ways. It's a great place to find out how you can volunteer to help homeless people.

1012 14th Street NW
Suite 600
Washington, D.C. 20005
202-737-6444
http://nch.ari.net

National Council on the Aging

The National Council on the Aging is devoted to helping seniors in many different ways. It's an excellent resource for finding out how to volunteer to help the elderly.

409 3rd Street SW
Washington, D.C. 20024
202-479-1200
www.ncoa.org

Oxfam America

Oxfam America helps fight poverty and social injustice throughout the world. It's particularly active in helping fight hunger and feed the hungry.

26 West Street
Boston, MA 02111
1-800-77OXFAM or 617-482-1211
www.oxfamamerica.org

The Salvation Army

The Salvation Army helps people in many ways, notably by feeding the hungry and providing shelters for the homeless. There are local branches in just about every community in the country.

1025 F Street NE
Washington, D.C. 20002
202-783-0233
www.salvationarmy.org

United Way of America

United Ways are local organizations across the country that help the needy, seniors, the hungry, and the homeless in many different ways. It's a great place to find volunteer opportunities to help the needy. Each United Way is run separately, but you can find one near you by checking the Yellow Pages or by contacting the national United Way of America.

701 North Fairfax Street
Alexandria, VA 22314
703-836-7112
www.unitedway.org

Resource Guide for Volunteering for Animals

Here are some of the best organizations you'll find to help you find a volunteer opportunity for working with animals.

American Society for the Prevention of Cruelty to Animals (ASPCA)

The ASPCA's mission is to "promote humane principles, prevent cruelty, and alleviate fear, pain, and suffering in animals." It's a national organization, with headquarters in New York City, and so the only volunteer opportunities it has are in New York. However, it's a great resource for finding shelters and the humane society in your local area. Its Web site, for example, has a listing of almost 5,000 local humane societies, SPCAs, shelters, and similar places to volunteer.

424 East 92nd Street
New York, NY 10128
212-876-7700
www.aspca.org

American Veterinary Medical Association

This is an organization of veterinarians. It's a great place to find out about animals and to find a veterinarian near you.

1931 North Meacham Road
Schaumburg, IL 60173
847-925-8070
www.avma.org

American Zoo and Aquarium Association

This group is the main association for zoos and aquariums across the country. Check it out to find local zoos and aquariums near you.

8403 Colesville Road
Suite 710
Silver Spring, MD 20910
www.aza.org

The Humane Society of the United States

This group calls itself the world's largest animal protection organization. It works in many ways to help animals, from helping local shelters to educating the public.

2100 L Street NW
Washington, D.C. 20037
212-452-1100
www.hsus.org

World Wildlife Fund

This is a worldwide organization devoted to protecting wildlife and wildlands. Check it out to find volunteer opportunities near you.

1250 24th Street NE
Washington, D.C. 20037
202-293-4800
www.worldwildlife.org

Resource Guide for Volunteering for the Environment

Here are some of the best organizations—both private groups and government organizations—to help you find a volunteer opportunity for the environment.

Environmental Defense Fund

This group fights for the environment in many different ways, and can help you find local volunteering opportunities.

257 Park Avenue South
New York, NY 10010
212-505-2100
www.edf.org

Environmental Protection Agency

This is the federal agency charged with enforcing environmental laws. It can also help you find volunteer opportunities with many other groups near you.

1200 Pennsylvania Avenue NW
Washington, D.C. 20460
www.epa.gov

Keep America Beautiful

This group works to fight litter and to promote recycling. It has many local programs, and probably has one near you.

1010 Washington Boulevard
Stamford, CT 06901
203-323-8987
www.kab.org

Kids for a Clean Environment Kids (F.A.C.E.)

Check this environmental kids' organization to find out how you can volunteer to help the environment.

P.O. Box 158254
Nashville, TN 37215
615-331-7381
www.kidsface.org

National Park Service

This federal agency runs the U.S. National Parks. There are many of them in every state, and not just in wilderness areas. Many cities, such as New York and Boston, also have areas run by the National Park Service. The National Park Service uses many volunteers.

1849 C Street NW
Washington, D.C. 20240
202-208-6843
www.nps.gov

National Wildlife Federation

This is one of the largest and most effective environmental organizations. It uses volunteers, and can also help you find volunteer opportunities near you.

8925 Leesburg Pike
Vienna, VA 22184
703-790-4000
www.nwf.org

Sierra Club

The Sierra Club is one of the oldest and best-known environmental organizations, with over 600,000 members. It has volunteer opportunities of its own, and will also guide you to other opportunities near you.

Sierra Club
Office of Volunteer and Activist Services
85 Second Street
San Francisco, CA 94105
www.sierraclub.com

The Student Conservation Association

This private group offers exceptional volunteer opportunities for teens. You'll do such things as build a cabin in Vermont's Merck Forest and Farmland Center or restore vegetation at campsites in Yosemite National Park.

P.O. Box 550
Charlestown, NH 03603
603-543-1700
www.sca-inc.org

Resource Guide for Volunteering to Build Better Neighborhoods

Here are some of the best organizations—both private groups and government organizations—to help you find a volunteer opportunity to build better neighborhoods.

AmeriCares

Among this group's many programs is AmeriCares Homefront, a program that helps repair homes across the country for those who need help.

161 Cherry Street
New Canaan, CT 06840
1-800-486-4357
www.americares.org

Christmas in April

This organization preserves and revitalizes housing and neighborhoods across the country for those who need help.

1536 16th Street NW
Washington, D.C. 20036
202-483-9081
www.christmasinapril.org

Habitat for Humanity International

This extraordinary group builds or rehabilitates housing for the needy across the country. The recipients of the homes work alongside volunteers to help build or rehabilitate their homes.

121 Habitat Street
Americus, GA 31709
1-800-HABITAT
www.habitat.org

Keep America Beautiful

This group works to fight litter and to beautify America. It has many local programs, and probably has one near you.

1010 Washington Boulevard
Stamford, CT 06901
203-323-8987
www.kab.org

Kids for a Clean Environment (Kids F.A.C.E.)

Check this environmental kids' organization to find out how you can volunteer to help clean up neighborhoods.

P.O. Box 158254
Nashville, TN 37215
615-331-7381
www.kidsface.org

U.S. Department of Housing and Urban Development (HUD)

This is the main federal agency that helps build better neighborhoods. It's also a great resource for finding volunteer opportunities not only with HUD, but with other groups as well.

451 7th Street SW
Washington, D.C. 20410
202-708-1112
www.hud.gov

Resource Guide for Volunteering for the Arts

Here are some of the best organizations for finding a volunteer opportunity in the arts.

National Endowment for the Arts

The National Endowment for the Arts is a federal agency that supports the arts in the United States. They give out grants to many local arts agencies and artists and so are an excellent resource for finding local arts organizations and museums near you.

1100 Pennsylvania Avenue NW
Washington, D.C. 20506
202-682-5400
www.nea.gov

National Endowment for the Humanities

The National Endowment for the Humanities is a federal agency that supports the humanities in the United States. They give out grants to many museums and arts agencies and so are an excellent resource for finding local arts organizations and museums near you.

1100 Pennsylvania Avenue NW
Washington, D.C. 20506
202-606-8400
www.neh.gov

Western States Arts Federation (WESTAF)

WESTAF is a non-profit organization dedicated to promoting and preserving the arts in Alaska, Arizona, California, Colorado, Idaho, Montana, Nevada, New Mexico, Oregon, Utah,

Washington, and Wyoming. It's also a great resource for finding local arts museums and organizations.

1543 Champa Street
Suite 220
Denver, CO 80202
303-629-1166
www.westaf.org

Resource Guide for Volunteering in Government and Politics

There are many, many thousands of government offices, political candidates, public interest groups, and advocacy groups. Use this guide to help find places to volunteer near you.

Democratic National Committee

This is the official organization of the Democratic party. It can help you find local Democratic candidates near you if you want to volunteer for them.

Democratic National Committee
430 S. Capitol Street SE
Washington, D.C. 20003
202-863-8000
www.democrats.org

League of Women Voters

This well-known organization educates people about public policy and encourages them to vote. It has chapters in many states and cities. If you have trouble finding your local chapter, call the national organization.

1730 M Street NW
Suite 1000
Washington, D.C. 20036
202-429-1965
www.lwv.org

Project Vote-Smart

This superb Web site, put together by volunteers, is one of the best resources to politics you'll find anywhere. It'll help you find the names and political leanings of your elected representatives so that you can decide who to volunteer for.

www.vote-smart.org

Republican National Committee

This is the official organization of the Republican party. It can help you find local Republican candidates near you if you want to volunteer for them.

310 1st Street SE
Washington, D.C. 20003
202-863-8500
www.rnc.org

Voter.com

Here's another Web site that's a great resource for everything to do with politics and government. It's particularly helpful for finding public interest and advocacy groups. Click on Activism to get a list of these groups.

www.voter.com

White House Online

The White House has an official Web site that's great for more than just finding information about the White House. It also has a comprehensive listing to just about every federal agency. Click on Gateway to Government for all the details.

www.whitehouse.gov

Resource Guide for Volunteering for Literacy and Education

Here are some of the best organizations you'll find to help you find a volunteer opportunity for literacy and education.

American Library Association

If you want any kind of information about libraries and literacy, here's the place to go.

50 E. Huron
Chicago, IL 60611
www.ala.org

Laubach Literacy Action

This literacy program helps 175,000 students every year in over 1,000 local organizations. It probably has one near you, and they need your help.

1320 Jamesville Avenue
Syracuse, NY 13210
1-888-LAUBACH or 315-422-9121
www.laubach.org

Literacy Volunteers of America

This program helps adults as well as their children, and has volunteering opportunities all across the country. Check the national headquarters to find an opportunity near you.

635 James Street
Syracuse, NY 13203
315-472-0001
www.literacyvolunteers.org

National Head Start Association

This is a national organization made up of the more than 2,000 Head Start organizations around the country. It's a great place to find out about Head Start programs and to find one near you.

1651 Prince Street
Alexandria, VA 22314
703-739-0875
www.nhsa.org

National Institute for Literacy

This organization has many programs that use volunteers. Call the toll-free number to find out about volunteer opportunities near you.

1-800-228-8813
www.nifl.org

Reading Is Fundamental (RIF)

This is perhaps the best organization anywhere for making sure that kids learn to read. Odds are there's a branch near you that needs your help.

1825 Connecticut Avenue NW
Suite 400
Washington, D.C. 20009
202-287-3196
www.rif.org

Books About Volunteering

If you're looking for more information about volunteering, check out these books:

Devney, Carcy Campion. *Volunteer's Survival Manual: The Only Practical Guide to Giving Your Time and Money* (The Practical Press, 1992). While this book is a bit outdated and written for adults rather than teens, it has some good advice for volunteers.

Duper, Linda Leeb. *160 Ways to Help the World: Community Service Projects for Young People* (Facts On File, Inc., 1996). Lots of ideas for teens on how to create your own volunteering opportunities.

Krannich, Ron, and Caryl Krannich. *Jobs and Careers with Non-Profit Organizations: Profitable Opportunities with Non-Profits* (Impact Publications, 1999). If you're thinking of getting serious about a career helping others, you'll find this a particularly valuable guide.

Lewis, Barbara A. *The Kid's Guide to Service Projects* (Free Spirit Publishing, 1995). While some of the projects you'll find in this book are a bit simplistic, it's still a very good resource if you want to come up with volunteer projects on your own.

Raynolds, John, with Gene Stone. *The Halo Effect: How Volunteering Can Lead to a More Fulfilling Life and a Better Career* (Golden Books, 1998). This book is aimed at adults who are working at other careers than volunteering. Still, you'll find some useful tidbits here.

Ryan, Jr., Bernard. *Community Service for Teens: Opportunities to Volunteer* (Ferguson Publishing Company, various publication dates). This is a series of eight books, with each book devoted to a single topic, such as protecting the environment or caring for animals. The books are a bit thin and a bit pricey, but they're very helpful.

Waldman, Jackie. *Teens with the Courage to Give* (Conari Press, 2000). This is an excellent book of inspiring stories, in teens' own words, of how kids overcame tragedies and went on to volunteer to help others.

Index

221

X–Z